[extra] Ordinary Miracles

Finding the miraculous amidst the mundane

[extra] Ordinary Miracles

Finding the miraculous amidst the mundane

A.B. Smithyman

INTEGRITY

MEDIA EUROPE

Integrity Media Europe
Unit 1 Hargreaves Business Park
Hargreaves Road
Eastbourne
BN23 6QW

www.worshipwithintegrity.com
www.iworship24-7.com

ISBN 978-1-907080-17-3
Typeset by Chris Coe
Printed and bound in the UK by CPI Anthony Rowe, Chippenham
and Eastbourne

Contents

Dedication

To my precious wife, whose heart and love has energised my steps in life. It is such an honour to be your husband and friend.

To the pilgrim, Alan Moore, who went to be with his Saviour in 2009. I may tend his physical garden from time to time, but his life's garden is continually displayed in the countless people he touched with his Father's great love.

r

What Others Are Saying About
[extra] Ordinary Miracles

The opportunity to look back into the lives of men and women touched by God's love is purposeful. The opportunity to then look up to God, the source of that amazing love, is precious. The opportunity to look at them together is powerful.

Reverend Katei Kirby
Communicator, mentor and Vice President of Tearfund

How can we resist the draining and distracting complexity of modern life? More than ever before do we need inspiration, encouragement and rest in God. With stories of how ordinary people, filled with the Spirit of God, have led extraordinary lives, these reflections provide refreshment for all us pilgrims. Supported by Scripture, quotes and prayer, they help to still our hearts, stimulate our minds and focus our gaze upon the beauty of the cross. They are fuel for disciples of Christ.

Dr David Landrum
Bible Society, Senior Parliamentary Officer,
House of Commons, London

This is a wonderful devotional. The format of timeless truths in thought-provoking reflections based on real people's lives, followed by a scripture, a quotation and a prayer, works really well. I was challenged and inspired by every one of the chapters.

Charles Whitehead
Chairman of the Catholic Evangelisation Services
Chairman of the International Charismatic Consultation
Co-Chairman of the UK Charismatic and
Pentecostal Leaders Conference

Andy's approach is fresh and brings us to a place where we can explore the issues and find answers. For personal or group use, this study really works.

Tom & Suzie Brock
Directors of Wave Of Life Ministries International

Andy Smithyman's book is my kind of book. Not being a big reader myself, it's the kind of book you can dip into and pick up pearls of wisdom and inspiration. It's great to have alongside your Bible for the morning quiet time.

Godfrey Birtill
Singer/songwriter

This lovely little book is both inspiring and sobering. Inspiring as we read of the amazing way the Lord has used the great and the humble, and sobering as we are reminded that God can use any life that is surrendered to him. Its chapters, scriptures and prayers are brief enough for it to be a helpful devotional aid in the rush and tumble of busy days.

John & Christine Noble
Speakers and Authors

Arranging historical vignettes, scriptural reflections and stories of everyday faithfulness, Andy Smithyman has composed a colorful kaleidoscope of life that will brighten your day and inspire your walk with God.

Marijke Hoek
Coordinator Forum For Change,
Evangelical Alliance

Foreword

This is an unusual book – what some would call a "devotional". It consists of 29 short chapters featuring a story related to revival, renewal or transformation, with carefully selected scriptures and an occasional quote from a writer or song lyricist.

Don't be afraid of that word – devotional. I write this especially for those who are starting out in life, the workplace or church leadership. I am an Evangelical Christian, and that means I am an activist – even at 65 years of age we are embarking on an exciting journey of church planting. Activity and busyness mark so many of our lives. But as I look back there has not been much time made simply to reflect and devote. We are not good at these things – just give us more things to do! But as I have often discovered, love for God's work, His Church and people can outgrow one's love for Christ.

We activists tend to have a list of people and issues to pray about – and most of us feel guilty that we do not pray enough! So maybe this small publication should be approached a day at a time, with space to read, reread and reflect further, as it encourages us towards devotion, love and affection, then maybe into thanks and forgiveness and even prayer for those who don't know Christ.

This will be our Pilgrim Journey: from busyness to the real business of feeding the soul, educating the mind and softening the heart. I hope this will not be the last we read of Andy Smithyman as he has done us activists a favour: to slow the pace for a while, to be fed, meditate and not consign such things to the elderly and pastoral.

This journey through the following pages will help us on the wider, longer and complex journey we engage in every day as we seek to make Christ attractive and intelligible. Enjoy the journey!

Gerald Coates
Founder of Pioneer
Author, speaker and broadcaster

Preface
Twenty-nine, Not Thirty

"Ordinary heroes, there's one on every street.
You may not recognise them, because they're just like you and me.
Ordinary heroes, you may not know their names.
Because they don't make the headlines,
but they are gonna save the day."

Ordinary Heroes, lyrics by Howard Jones
(D-TOX Records, 2009)

What you are about to read started as a journey many years ago. I guess you could track it back to my childhood days when I sat with my father and mother, listening to them recount testimonies of how God was moving across the lands. They taught me to value the importance of stories and, more so, the individuals within them. As those childhood days turned into adult devotion and study, I continued to seek out similar stories and eventually began interviewing people and recording some of my own. In time, a passion best described as "finding the hidden gems" emerged in me.

In amongst the bookshelves of our homes and local stores lies a wealth of stories told of people who believed in their Lord – lives that history chose to publicly record, bringing our attention to their deeds and efforts. Some exist in the form of biographies, like those of famous revivalists or community leaders, while others are found in our Bibles in passages such as the list of the heroes of faith in Hebrews 11.

There is great beauty and rightful prominence in these public lives. They are accounts that deserve our honour and respect and from which we can gather encouragement and learning for our own walk of faith. Yet, as the observer is captured by the work of God's hand upon such lives, another series of tones and shades begin to appear within His masterpiece of life – differing strands of interweaving stories, not so noticeable until one looks closely, but that reveal a togetherness of equal worth and significance.

Whether in the Scriptures or the side remarks made in the journals and letters of heroes of faith, paying homage to lesser-known characters who have served sacrificially, we can find a chorus of applause that leads us to look beyond the individual to the "togetherness" that we all contribute towards – the togetherness of God's great love.

This can be displayed in many differing ways. Occasionally our service to Christ will find welcome in the high acclaim of fame. But more often we are called as gentle pilgrims to travel paths out of sight from any earthly praise – to be one of God's hidden gemstones in the land, contributing selfless acts of love to all those around us.

In the following pages then, you will read about characters both named and unnamed, whose lives take us past the pursuit of any title or position. Instead, the steps they left, or are still leaving in this world, create the shape of the One they love, with hints of some of the values that they hold dear. Some come from the history books we read, some from interviews that have been conducted over the years of my own soul journey. But all are just a fraction of the countless pilgrims that surround our lives each day.

As I neared the completion of this book, I visited some close friends who asked me how the writing was going. I proceeded to give them a quick run down on my progress and ended with the comment that I had about 29 draft chapters complete and all that was left was to write just one more. Their response was to ask, "Why 30 chapters? Are you trying to round up the numbers?" I laughed as I nodded in response. It was exactly what I was trying to do. 30 was a nice tidy number compared to the odd and (perceived) incomplete 29. Surely it makes a much smarter and expected finish having "30 reflective readings"?

I never did write that 30th chapter. It seemed fitting for this work to carry a little unexpectedness, echoing the lives that influenced its journey. These characters challenge how things are seen and encourage us to re-evaluate what we ourselves have within: jewels of heavenly worth that sometimes don't conform to the standards of this world, but in their perceived incompleteness, carry the unique and genuine completeness of the One we all truly love.

1: Our Love Song

"Here is love, vast as the ocean.
Loving-kindness as the flood,
When the Prince of Life, our Ransom,
Shed for us His precious blood.
Who His love will not remember?
Who can cease to sing His praise?
He can never be forgotten.
Throughout Heaven's eternal days."

*Here is Love, words by William Rees (1802-83),
translated from Welsh to English by William Edwards
in The Baptist Book of Praise (1900)*

Stories of the 1904 Welsh awakening still warm, stir and provoke countless hearts. Built on the momentum of previous moves of God, this time in history is recorded by many diverse accounts. It was a time when the cry of salvation echoed throughout Wales in a transforming move of God that changed lives, business infrastructures and sporting events to name but a few things. There are also many wonderful stories about the signs and wonders that sparked a fire to countries beyond its shores. Yet entwined within such acts that capture our enthusiasm stands the hymn, "Here is Love". During this period of time it was known as the "love song" of the revival.

Many characters contributed to this piece of history, both prior, during, and after the awakening's most famous individual, Evan Roberts. One of them is a lady called Annie Davies, an 18-year old who would travel with a band of singing women and minister alongside the famous preacher. Her rendition of this hymn would often move a congregation to tears. Its lines, sung outside drinking houses and clubs, would usher men outside to find salvation. Though some, at the time, raised questions about women taking such an active part in revival meetings, Annie and her friend's commitment and enthusiasm encouraged many women to step into more prominent roles.

These lyrics of a Baptist minister who loved to write poetry, combined with the voice of a young lady who was able to capture the essence of the words written, were brought to life in a vivid realisation of God's love. Joining with her, a collective chorus of broken voices from all backgrounds and status' congregated at the foot of the cross to sing in heartfelt worship, "On the mount of crucifixion, fountains opened deep and wide. Through the floodgates of God's mercy, flowed a vast and gracious tide." The words sung by Annie had such power and impact because here was someone who was enraptured by the presence of God.

One of the most precious moments I have ever experienced was with a small group of people who had lived through a revival that took place in 1949. They had continued to pray together regularly and offered an open door to anyone who wanted to join in with them. It was a prayer meeting of deep conviction with words filled with tears and groans that came from the very depth of their souls – something I have never heard before or since.

You would expect that inner cry to be about a desire to see, once again, the miracles and wonders of old. But instead their eyes filled with tears of devotion as they tried to explain what it meant to live a life where you felt the presence of God in so many tangible ways. The touch of God's hand had moved each person past the famous stories and events to find a home in the deep realisation of His love, where all one's works, goals and talents are gladly laid prostrate at the foot of the cross.

These people had encountered the reality of the overwhelming love of God and since that moment their lives had never been the same. The blood that flowed through their veins carried the unmistakable DNA of the Holy One and their vision was firmly centred upon the greatest love story of all: God's love for you and me. "Of Thy fullness Thou art pouring, Thy great love and power on me. Without measure, full and boundless. Drawing out my heart to Thee."

A love song of revival is something more than a tribute to the stories of wonder. It goes beyond the vast congregations and famous sermons of old. It weaves in and out of all our expectations and settles upon the timeless truth that we are loved – loved so deeply that He gave His only Son. Loved so much, that He didn't think it an injustice to become a servant for redemption.

There really is no better place to be. Christ's beautiful love song over us, forever priceless and continually remembered, speaks "throughout Heaven's eternal days".

Moments to reflect

"The person who refuses to love doesn't know the first thing about God, because God is love – so you can't know Him if you don't love.
This is how God showed His love for us;
God sent His only Son into the world so we might live through Him.
This is the kind of love we are talking about – not that we once upon a time loved God,
but that He loved us and sent His Son as a sacrifice
to clear away our sins and the damage they've done in our relationship with God."

(1 John 4:8-10 The Message)

"Now, I am singing all day long
the praises of His blood;
No other theme awakes my song
Like Calv'rys crimson flood."

Evans Roberts, Diary Entry 31st September 1904

Prayer:

"Let me be forever captivated by Your love song, Lord; forever held in its embrace. Thank You that I am cherished and adored, bought from sin with such a price. Let the reality of that cost never once leave my central gaze. Let its truth continually run throughout this life's vein, where my actions and lifestyle always speak of Your love to this world. No fancy lights or extravagant presentations will ever compare to this great story of hope: of a universal, creating God, choosing me in desire and perfect love."

2: The Worth of You

"This above all: to thine own self be true,
And it must follow, as the night the day,
Thou canst not then be false to any man."

William Shakespeare, Hamlet Act 1, scene 3

The Azusa Street Revival is an event in history familiar to many groupings of our faith – an event famously captured and preserved in its location and date: 312 Azusa Street, 14th April, 1906. There we find William J. Seymour, along with a small congregation, moving into a disused building with a diverse history. It had previously been an African Methodist Episcopal Church, a warehouse, a lumberyard, a tombstone shop and even stables with rented rooms above.

Frequent and spontaneous meetings took place, regardless of the time of day, attracting many visitors from differing ages, races and backgrounds. While the majority of the country still operated racial segregation, these meetings saw a blending of all races sitting, praying and worshipping together. As Frank Bartleman so perfectly observed: "The colour line was washed away in the Blood." The gatherings also furthered the cause of the empowerment of women that was already happening within local congregations. With women's right to vote still some years away, here both genders occupied clear leadership positions.

This move continued for many years, slowly ebbing away between 1913 and 1915. But its effects had already caused a continued ripple throughout the nations. While it also brought criticism and questions surrounding the manifestations that were happening – some of it well founded – the fruit of this work saw many missionaries rise up and preach the Gospel in both their home country and abroad.

A quick glance over these monumental dates, highlight many linked events. In February 1906, Seymour had arrived in Los Angeles by the invitation of a lady called Neely Terry. She wanted him to preach at the local church she was attending. But, following his sermon on the gift of tongues, Seymour found himself padlocked from the building by the elders of the church.

Edward S. Lee, who was a member of that congregation, took him into his home. He prayed and fasted with Seymour, joining with him on his knees in pursuit for God's power and touch upon their lives. A small group developed and they eventually moved into 214, North Bonnie Brae Street. It is here we find the famous account of the baptism of the Holy Spirit on April 9th 1906, where in the middle of a time of fasting, Edward S. Lee first spoke in tongues.

The lives of Neely and Edward are ones to encourage us all. Mixing their lives between the routine of daily work and their care for the home, they contributed their individual tones into the wider symphony that God was orchestrating. A simple act of an invitation, a loving gesture of an open home, and a sacrificial commitment to prayer. All these brought forth results that echo throughout history.

The mirror that the world uses to reflect the worth and contribution of individuals can easily mislead us into thinking that certain offerings are minimal and insignificant. This is not the case. Christ continually hints at the wonderful gemstones of miracles within the normality our faith's walk.

Your life is a worshipful offering that carries great beauty and utmost significance. It is not founded on any self-grading of importance, but firmly placed upon His love for you and your love for Him. With that understanding, whatever simple thing you do for Him shines forth His name in glorious rays.

Moments to reflect

"You're blessed when you're at the end of your rope.
With less of you there is more of God and His rule.
You're blessed when you feel you've lost what is most dear to you.
Only then can you be embraced by the One most dear to you.
You're blessed when you're content with just who you are –
no more, no less.
That's the moment you find yourselves proud owners of everything
that can't be bought.
You're blessed when you've worked up a good appetite for God.
He's food and drink in the best meal you'll ever eat.
You're blessed when you care.
At the moment of being 'care-full', you will find yourselves cared for.
You're blessed when you get your inside world – your mind and heart –
put right.
Then you can see God in the outside world."

(Matthew 5:3-8 The Message)

"There came a sound from Heaven, as a mighty rushing wind. It filled their hearts with singing, and gave them peace within. The Master gave this promise, He said the Spirit will descend. And from your inner being, a river with no end."

There Is A River, words and Music by Max and
David Sapp © 1969.

Prayer:

"Thank You, Father, that I am of worth. I can hear You sing this over me. My life, created by Your loving hands, contains priceless fragments of You. You encourage me to be myself, true to what You placed within. The tones that carry my individuality play in creation's symphony. Each gifting, each leisure time hobby, whether through work or fun-filled play, reveals Your intricate workmanship, so delicately shaped with loving care. Help me to live daily in astounding certainty of Your complete and comprehensive love."

3: A Pearl of Refined Beauty

*"Praise be to the God and Father of our Lord Jesus Christ!
In His great mercy, He has given us new birth into a living hope
through the resurrection of Jesus Christ from the dead, and into
an inheritance that can never perish, spoil or fade – kept in
heaven for you, who through faith are shielded by God's power
until the coming of salvation that is ready to be revealed in the
last time. In this you greatly rejoice, though now for a little while
you may have to suffer grief in all kinds of trials. These have come
so that your faith - of greater worth than gold, which perishes
even though refined by fire – may be proved genuine and may
result in praise, glory and honour when Jesus Christ is revealed."*

(1 Peter 1:3-7 NIV)

It seems a mystery of our pilgrimage that, attached so closely
to our steps of joy and satisfaction, are the footprints of trials
and sacrifice. Frequently these steps are not fully explained or
reasoned out, but something of wonder happens as we tread
their path: the slow but sure purifying of our faith on God's
anvil that enhances the ongoing craftsmanship of our life,
refining a beauty that is deep within.

There was a family living in the East of England whose lives
constantly communicated this refining fire, yet they never uttered
a word about it. They faithfully served in their community, helping
those around them, while keeping up with a 9-5 job. They had
no ministry organisation around them to gather support; there
was no charity payroll or Gift Aid claims. It was just them: a
husband, a wife and two young children.

Their history was laden with trials of finance, pressures of
time, and misunderstood actions, as they continued to devote

much of their resources to helping their neighbours. The father regularly heard statements saying he wasn't being the "man" that he should be, providing financial security for his family. The mother's regular trips to the school gate became a mocking fashion show as her clothes were looked down upon by many around her. Together they experienced the pain that only loving parents can, as they saw their children's equipment falling short of the ever-changing demands of childhood competition, whilst remaining unable to do anything about it.

Their lives of service, readily embracing personal sacrifice to put their neighbours before themselves, demonstrated God's presence in the everydayness of their lives. Yes, they had questions that remained unanswered; yes, there were terrible valley experiences as well as times of high praise; yes, there were moments when they could not understand what was happening. But through it all their testimony and example declared that God was faithful.

That faithfulness shone through their lives with such radiant beauty, that no carefully prepared set of words upon this page can adequately describe it. And while they weren't put on pedestals or mentioned in congregational bulletins, the precious wealth they contained within was visually evident as you walked up and down the streets with them. It was apparent as they delivered a meal to a person who lived in the darkness of perpetually closed curtains and as they pushed an envelope full of cash through the letterbox of a family they knew were struggling to pay their gas bill. This lifestyle of love continued as they welcomed their own reduced shopping trolley, making sure an extra basket was full for their neighbour who had just recently lost his job. All these seemingly "small" acts mounted up to a treasure of heavenly beauty.

This is but one example of the personal sacrifices that can find residence in the hearts of many travelling pilgrims. We walk a path made of stones of joy, joined together with the cement of trials and endurance. We cannot map such a journey or blueprint it with a formula. It flows out of God's work in the unique personality of every believer as He continues to shape our life and carries the familiar hallmark of the cross that we hold so dear.

God has placed a pearl of priceless beauty within each of us. It is being refined with each step we take. Sometimes it is unseen by our own human eye, yet amazingly it is recognised by those around us. We pronounce His name, declaring His beauty through our lives in ways that no words can express.

That is one of the marvels of this journey of faith that we walk. We can never underestimate the pearl of beauty we carry – the very presence of God.

Moments to reflect

"Dear friends,
do not be surprised at the painful trial you are suffering,
as though something strange were happening to you.
But rejoice that you participate in the sufferings of Christ,
so that you may be overjoyed when His glory is revealed."
(1 Peter 4:12-13 NIV)

"Sometimes He comes in the rain.
And we question the pain,
and wonder why God can seem so far away.
But time will show us,
He was right there with us.
Sometimes He comes in the clouds.
Sometimes His face cannot be found.
Sometimes the sky is dark and grey.

But some things can only be known.
And sometimes He comes in the clouds."

Sometimes He Comes In the Clouds by Steven Curtis Chapman
(based upon Oswald Chambers' My Utmost For His Highest)
Copyright: 1995 Word Entertainment LLC, a Warner/Curb Company

Prayer:

"What comfort engulfs me to know that You are continually working with my life! Through both bellows of laughter and tears of pain, Your loving embrace is ever near. To follow You seems foolish to worldly gain, but steps of promise find hope within the Refiner's fire. Deliver me from seeking any trophy to display from the cost I have counted in this precious walk. Shape my life to see Your world around me. Let Your love shine brightly through this life so dearly in love with You."

4: Our Great Expectation

"The morning finds me here a heaven's door.
A place I've been so many times before.
Familiar thoughts and phrases start to flow.
And carry me to places that I know so well.
And do I dare remember where I am.
I stand before the great eternal throne.
The one that God Himself is seated on.
And I, I've been invited as a son.
I've been invited to come and
Believe the unbelievable,
Receive the inconceivable,
And see beyond my wildest imagination.
Lord, I come with great expectations."

Great Expectation by Steven Curtis Chapman (Sparrow, 1999)

There is a wealth to be amazed at as we consider the wondrous elegance of this great invitation – an invitation that cannot be fully explained in human words or even great works of art. It baffles our logic and confuses the wise. Yet it captures our heart in simple grandeur: that the universal creating God invites us to commune with Him.

An elderly lady called Maud first hinted to me about this precious gift of intimate communion. Her skirts showed signs of wear – marks of time spent upon her knees. Her eyesight was failing. Yet her vision was set upon something as clear as the brightest of days. This lady's history was wrapped up in many stories of God moving, but her excitement was set upon something far away from the most glamorous of accounts.

In the years following her death, I have grown to appreciate many of the pearls of beauty that Maud spoke of so often. But the one that stands out above every other is this priceless gift of intimacy with God.

It is not with a great fanfare that this beautiful invitation is received. There is no dress code or protocol we can follow to be accepted. We have to do no more than seek His presence. Scholars, writers and painters have all tried to capture this moment, but all have fallen short. There is richness in His presence that goes beyond imagination and yet confounds us with its beauty and simplicity. It is the love and joy of a Father expressed to His child, an intimacy during which the inconceivable riches of salvation are whispered into our ears.

But how quickly do such special moments become a routine? Has dwelling in His presence become an act of normality that we take for granted as we multi-task our way through life's schedule? And yet, we want such occasions to be our "normal". There is great strength in coming to Him not as a special occasion, but in the everydayness of our daily life. We are free to come to Him without ceremony. The barriers of position, rank and protocol have all been removed – we can rest, move, dance and sing in His presence.

Yes, we can come to God in the normality of our existence, for this is our freedom in Christ – a truly wondrous and beautiful present and future hope. But the relative ease with which we can find a quiet corner to pray in or flick through scriptures can also clothe us in a heavy cloak of indifference. Familiar words and phrases all too easily slip off our tongue and make time in His presence all too commonplace. Our intimacy can become mundane as we work through a set of pre-prepared words. The steps of our dance can belie a remembered routine instead of a spontaneous display of our joy.

We need to lay our heads on the Lord's chest and hear His heartbeat afresh as we re-examine our approach to His presence. No matter how easy it is for us to enter or to let familiar words come from our mouth, we need to pause and think about the magnitude of this invitation, recapturing our first love – a love that is beyond any time schedule; a love that puts our life story into perspective; a love that puts everything else on pause.

And as we rest in His arms, and as we move in this great dance of communion, we hear His words whisper in our ears once again. This is our invitation to commune with great expectation.

Moments to reflect

"Who, being in very nature God,
did not consider equality with God something to be grasped,
but made himself nothing,
taking the very nature of a servant,
being made in human likeness.
And being found in appearance as a man,
he humbled himself and became obedient to death –
even death on a cross!
Therefore God exalted him to the highest place
and gave him the name that is above every name,
that at the name of Jesus every knee should bow,
in heaven and on earth and under the earth,
and every tongue confess that Jesus Christ is Lord,
to the glory of God the Father."

(Philippians 2:6-11 NIV)

"May all your expectations be frustrated.
May all your plans be thwarted.
May all your desires be withered into nothingness.
That you may experience the powerlessness and poverty of a child

and sing and dance in the compassion of God who is Father, Son and Spirit.

Amen."

Brennan Manning, Closing Prayer

Prayer:

"Precious Lord, what a wonder it is to know Your presence, feel Your embrace and hear Your words. You confound my wildest thoughts. Let me never lose sight of the journey that led me to this intimate dance – the footsteps of the One who has forever shaped my heart. Nothing can repay such a priceless gift. But You ask for no such payment. Instead you simply call me to be caught up in Your whirlwind of love and adoration – to be an adult in brokenness as my gaze falls upon the cross and a child in simplicity as I run into Your arms, My loving Father and Creator of the universe."

5: Mosaic Love

"This kind of Christian fellowship I had never seen,
nor ever thought of seeing on earth.
It fully reminded me of what I had read in the Holy Scriptures,
of the primitive Christians who loved each other and broke bread,
in partaking of it from house to house."

Olaudah Equiano, Rough Crossing
(freed slave, writer) describing a congregational meeting in 1774

The Gospel of Christ is something of immense beauty. It is a light that shines with a brightness so unique and distinctive that no work of forgery can bear the scrutiny of its radiance. It contains a purity unspoilt by human hands and selfish agendas. It carries such worth that even the casual passer-by cannot avoid an intake of breathe.

No matter what we build around it – structures, uniforms, approach to gender, age and practice – the magnificence of the Gospel outshines our greatest ideas. We could construct the most exquisite of buildings, pave its floors with gold and hang it with striking paintings and images of our Saviour and it would in no way compare with the simple, humble, but utterly compelling attractiveness of our God saying that He loves us.

For many, regardless of whether they claim to be a follower of Christ or an ardent atheist, the "Blessed Mother Teresa of Calcutta" is the most credible example of love in action. Founding a humble missionary work in India in 1950, then gathering wider recognition in the 1970's, she was a clear reflection of Christ's compassion. Her life was an open sermon that convicted many to examine their own. Even though she expressed doubts about her faith at times, when exposed to such great poverty, her heart always found solace with her Saviour.

"Where did [she] find the strength and perseverance to place herself completely at the service of others? She found it in prayer and in the silent contemplation of Jesus Christ, His Holy Face, His Sacred Heart."

From the familiar to the unfamiliar – there are countless other examples of compassion; people whose names are not known to the masses, but who also gave countless years of service with the aim of expressing the love of Christ to others. One of these is Susan Conroy. In her EWTN talk, "Speaking of Saints" she recounts her time in Calcutta and how she was overwhelmed with the pain she saw around her. Sitting by the bed of someone who was terminally ill, she saw her fellow Sisters giving comfort to others, using their gifts and talents to help each patient in those dying moments. Initially, Susan felt like she had nothing to give, comparing her abilities with her fellow Sisters. But then the moment came when she simply held the hand of a dying patient. Then she realised that what she could give was the simple act of love.

Love is central to all that we are. It provides us with a purpose and a clarity to our journey. God's love is gloriously non-hierarchical. A cup of water offered to one thirsty person holds the same amount of compassion as a soup kitchen program serving two hundred. Taking someone into our home and providing shelter for them carries equal weight with God as launching an award-winning night hostel initiative. Such acts of love speak of our heart entwined with His, captured in His embrace. His life flows through our veins and is outworked through our steps. Our service in life is part of a tapestry, interweaving stories of His love expressed towards His world.

"He is jealous for me. Love's like a hurricane, I am a tree. Bending beneath the weight of His wind and mercy . . . and I realise just how beautiful You are and how great Your affections are for me."

In this world where ideas flow like water, fast-moving like a river, there is something beautiful in the simple truth of love. Whether we win a Nobel Peace Prize or sit with a dying person, gently holding their hand, love's language speaks the same. It communicates the value we carry, the value that comes from being loved by the Holy One. Our actions, no matter how great or small, contribute to the mosaic picture the world will see – the undeniable image of His great love.

Moments to reflect

"If I speak in the tongues of men and of angels,
but have not love, I am only a resounding gong or a clanging cymbal.
If I have the gift of prophecy and can fathom all mysteries and
all knowledge,
and if I have a faith that can move mountains,
but have not love, I am nothing.
If I give all I possess to the poor and surrender my body to the flames,
but have not love, I gain nothing.
Love is patient, love is kind.
It does not envy, it does not boast, it is not proud.
It is not rude, it is not self-seeking,
it is not easily angered, it keeps no record of wrongs.
Love does not delight in evil, but rejoices with the truth.
It always protects, always trusts,
always hopes, always preserves."

(1 Corinthians 13:1-7 NIV)

"So we are His portion and He is our prize.
Drawn to redemption by the grace in His eyes.
If grace is an ocean we're all sinking.
So heaven meets earth like a sloppy wet kiss,
and my heart turns violently inside my chest . . .
Oh, how He loves us."

How He Loves by John Mark McMillan © 2005.

Prayer:

"Father God, set my heart alight with Your love and consume it with Your life. I welcome Your purifying fire as You work to make Your beauty increasingly shine from my life. Help me not to look at my actions as a means of calculating my worth, but keep my eyes fixed on Your glory. Help me never to pursue recognition, but rather be driven by Your compassion. Thank You that I am loved, cherished and adored, not because of any works that I do, but simply because You are in love with me. Help me demonstrate that love to others in practical ways."

6: His Imprint of Infinite Possibilities

"Lucy felt a little frightened, but she felt very inquisitive and excited as well. She looked back over her shoulder and there, between the dark tree trunks, she could see the open doorway of the wardrobe and even catch a glimpse of the empty room from which she had set out."

C.S. Lewis, The Lion, the Witch and the Wardrobe

C.S. Lewis seems to have captured the allure of mystery perfectly. The imagery of a big house full of rules and regulations, a childhood game of hide-and-seek, and the stumbling across a wardrobe that opens up into a whole new world. Imagine if we were part of that story, walking past the coats and hangers, then gazing upon that unknown land. What would go through our minds as we beheld that vast landscape and then turned back to see the reality of the wardrobe? Would we get hung up on how a wooden clothes box should function, or find excitement in what lay to be discovered?

Mystery is a wonderful gift from God. On our hearts He has engraved an invitation, daring us to allow our lives to be engulfed by His infinite possibilities. In our pursuit of growing spiritually, we too can become like children, lost in an ever-evolving landscape. We are invited by God to embark on an adventure where no mountain is too high to climb, or ocean too vast to cross. It is a world where our imagination becomes reality, because with God, everything we assumed about the "normal" way of doing things has changed.

Yet, we live in between the continual struggle of what we know and what we dare to dream. We live constantly in transition, desiring to run with childhood freedom, but acknowledging the adult "rules of the house" – rules that exist to give us boundaries, rules that speak of common sense and of being for our good. Such boundaries are not wrong. Far from it, they comfort and guide us. But sometimes rules take on another form and become manmade holy statues that must not be touched. They bind us instead of releasing us.

Maybe we have been told that we are too young to think the way we do, or too old to run this race effectively any more? Maybe we've been told that our gender or our education is a barrier to our dreams? Maybe we have looked at others who we consider much more gifted than us and been overwhelmed, unhelpfully comparing our own modest gifts and abilities? Worse still, maybe we look in the mirror each day and see staring back at us a litany of past mistakes and failures, and we assume that this disqualifies us from achieving our purpose in Christ? Here is something amazing: none of these things matter to God, who does not disqualify us, but instead changes the rules and beckons us towards the wardrobe.

For many years, a Swiss lady prayed for God to move within her adopted country of France. One of the answers to this longing came in the form of an Englishman named Douglas R. Scott. From his initial visit in 1927, and then his return in 1930, Douglas and his French wife, Clarice Weston, felt the Holy Spirit prompting them to become missionaries to this European country and beyond. What shines out from their story is that we are all pilgrims with infinite possibilities if we surrender to God and allow Him to do His miraculous work.

Douglas was not the best French speaker, but he and his wife's decision to pursue their journey of faith contributed to the wonderful wider story of God's hand upon that nation. His friend Dr. Lester Sumrall explained it this way: "No human being has ever chopped up the French language as badly as Douglas Scott, but he was so innocent in it that the people roared with laughter. He would say things he did not mean to say simply by mispronouncing the language. But when he laid hands on people, they were healed."

How releasing it is for us to know that nothing is too big for our God. No person's situation is irredeemable and He has ways of doing things that turn our expectations upside down. He can plant a dream into someone's life to spread His message of love to France, and not be restricted by any lack of eloquence in that person's grasp of the language. In fact that very weakness – just like a widow's modest jar of oil or a little boy's lunch of fish and bread – can become the vehicle through which His marvellous works are declared to many.

Our wonderful, creative God has planted so much wealth within us. He gives us dreams that will result in lives that shine with His glory. Some are great dreams, some less ambitious. It's not about size; it could be reaching a nation or helping our neighbours to touch our community. All that matters is that we dare to step into God's wardrobe and see what He will open up before us.

Just like the childhood game of hide and seek, our God urges us to become like children again, and invites us to play with Him and run, darting from one space to the next, trying to uncover the clues He has left for us. Somehow, in ways only He can, He orchestrates our steps so that we bump into the wardrobe and are confronted with the opportunity to step into our destiny. It may well defy our logic, but He will help us to see what it means to live with His glorious fingerprints on the infinite possibilities of our dreams.

Moments to reflect

"The people brought children to Jesus, hoping He might touch them.
the disciples shooed them off.
But Jesus was irate and let them know it:
'Don't push these children away. Don't ever get between them and Me.
These children are at the very centre of life in the Kingdom.
Mark this: Unless you accept God's Kingdom in the simplicity of a child,
you'll never get in.'
Then, gathering the children up in His arms,
He laid His hands of blessing on them."

(Mark 10:13-16 The Message)

"Tannen's Mystery Magic Box ...
15 dollars buys you 50 dollars worth of magic.
If you look at this, you'll see that it's never been opened.
But I've had this forever.
And I realised that I haven't opened it
because it represents something important to me.
... it represents infinite possibility.
Now it's not the most groundbreaking idea, but maybe there are times
where mystery is more important than knowledge."

J.J. Abrams, Mystery Box Talk at TED

Prayer:

"Father God, help me to be like a child in your presence, full of love and imagination; where any knowledge I have gained or status I have earned in life, never stops me from daring to dream. Help me learn to dwell in your presence where your works and purpose for my life will be outworked. May I always cherish a life of discovery, and never look down on simple belief. Thank You that in You, all my dreams and desires are fulfilled."

7: There Is More To Thomas

*"'But Rabbi,' they said. 'A short while ago they tried to stone you,
and yet you are going back there?' Jesus went on to tell them, 'Our
friend Lazarus has fallen asleep but I am going there to wake him
up.' His disciples replied, 'Lord if he sleeps, he will get better.'
So Jesus told them plainly. 'Lazarus is dead, and for your sake
I am glad I was not there, so that you may believe.' Then
Thomas said to the rest of the disciples, 'Let us also go,
that we may die with Him.'"*

(John 11:8-16 NIV)

Thomas is a disciple that seems to be best remembered for
his doubting of the resurrected Christ. That remembrance is
further reinforced by the retelling of that moment through our
religious paintings, Sunday School re-enactments and Easter
sermons. Yet, wrapped up in his story is a wonderful account of
how he dared to follow His Lord, even if it meant death. And
with that act of commitment, he encouraged the remaining
disciples to follow their own journeys with the Saviour.

One of the main insights such humble characters of our faith
teach us, is that respect and honour are values that are intimately
woven into our worship and walk with God. To simply live
a life of integrity, before God and with each other, is perhaps
the greatest virtue. In that sense we no longer need to pick out
fragmented moments from each other's lives on which we judge
one another, but see a "complete" life in Christ.

Described in differing ways but always pointing to the same
theme, many of these pilgrims elude to a journey we would all
benefit from taking. It is implied in the life of every saint that

there is a journey ahead of us they won't explain fully, since it would spoil the whole journey for us. But each person leaves traces, hints and clues, that make us look beyond the mountain-tops and valleys of their life and soak in the whole landscape before us. Instead of focusing on the grass, the trees or the hills, we detect the life that blows through the landscape like the wind of the Spirit, swaying each leaf and blade of grass with its presence. When we look differently, we see a vista open up before us that was hidden until now.

What a beautiful image those hints allude to – the deep truth that a person's life goes beyond digestible summaries and headline moments. It diverts our attention away from the mountain-top and valley experiences and broadens our gaze to see the swirls and currents of life.

This is the dimension that many wonderful pilgrims of Christ have seen: a different lens through which they observed their fellow travellers. Not condoning or condemning certain actions, but reflecting upon life's landscape with honesty and respect. Understanding that beneath the frailty of one's life lies His Spirit, working through each earthen vessel. Knowing that they too have feet of clay that lead them to continually come back to the realization of the love of Christ upon their lives – not just recalling the moment of salvation, but a deep knowing of their daily need for His mercy that is never shaken. A recognition that throughout all their years, they had good times of success and challenging experiences of failure. Times when they ran with great energy holding the banner of Christ, and times when they hid deep in shame of their sin or mistake. Yet each day didn't alter His love for them. He was always there, always listening, always showing that their life was more than just the obvious, visible moments.

And that is why they only hint and not fully explain this journey before us. Because to fall down before His mercy seat cannot be taught, only experienced. It scars our life with a constant memory of our need for Him, leaving us with a limp in our walk that dislodges us from any of our fleshly support mechanisms. History, jobs and titles all seem to fade as His great love is revealed, declaring we are more to Him than our actions and deeds. That regardless of the heights and depths we have travelled, we still acknowledge that we carry His treasure in a clay jar. That changes everything, including how we see each other and all the footprints we leave behind.

Thomas is remembered for another thing as well: he is the Apostle, tradition relates, who took the Gospel to Asia, Africa, Europe and India. Yet observing his life through the lens of these pilgrims speaks of an assurance that is as beautiful as it is powerful. It reveals to us that no single chapter in our life's account adequately portrays who we are. Often our experiences are simply "paragraphs" in the much larger novel of our lives. Sometimes these paragraphs recount time when we doubted God and wanted further confirmation. At other times they recall our firm conviction and strong belief. Only in the complete unfolding of our story do we see the picture of completeness in the light of God's love, grace and continual commitment to us that is being written on every single page.

Moments to reflect

"Instead, speaking the truth in love,
we will in all things grow up into Him who is the Head, that is, Christ.
From Him the whole body, joined and held together by every
supporting ligament,
grows and builds itself up in love,
as each part does its work."

(Ephesians 4:15-16 NIV)

"How can I say thanks for the things You have done for me?
Things so undeserved, yet You gave to prove Your love for me.
The voices of a million angels, could not express my gratitude.
All that I am, and ever hope to be.
I owe it all to Thee.
To God be the glory, to God be the glory.
To God be the glory, for the things He has done."

To God Be The Glory by Andrae Crouch
Warner Bros/Wea © 1996

Prayer:

"Thank you, precious Saviour, that Your treasure resides within this earthen vessel. Indescribable in any attempted description is Your loving commitment to this life of mine. May your love and mercy never depart from my sight as I walk this life with fellow pilgrims. Let the touch of Your presence leave its mark on me. I owe all of my life to You."

8: Outside The Frame

"There's a wideness in God's mercy, I cannot find in my own.
And He keeps His fire burning, to melt this heart of stone.
Keeps me aching with a yearning, keeps me glad
to have been caught.
In the reckless raging fury, that they call the love of God.

Now I've seen no band of angels, but I've heard the soldiers' songs.
Love hangs over them like a banner, love within them
leads them on.
To the battle on the journey, and it's never gonna stop.
Ever widening their mercies, and the fury of His love."

Love of God by Rich Mullins (Reunion © 1993)

There is a well-known quote that says "the camera never lies". We know what that means, yet the reality often proves different. A carefully thought out angle can alter what we see, by leading our eye to focus in on a certain perspective and obscuring other details outside of the shot. A simple photo-editing program can change skin tone, remove blemishes and present a portrait of beauty that is actually fictitious.

Then, the addition of other emotive images within a shot can elicit particular emotions and highlight something the photographer wants to emphasise, directing our attention down a certain path. The motives for doing any of these things could be myriad, but the fact is, the camera certainly does not tell the whole story.

The marriage of an "image" and our "interpretation" of it is something that constantly defines the boundaries of our lives. Our lifestyle choices, our politics, even our views on eschatology, as well as the entire wealth of our personal history and experience all combine together to influence how we see and interpret the world. They build a lens through which we observe and then filter life's "images" into a building block of meanings that we can understand and relate to.

We don't easily consider things that fall outside of the frame of our unique life lens, but God – and other characters we encounter on our journey – frequently challenge us to. One such character is the unnamed man who connected with the life of famous 19th century preacher Billy Bray.

William "Billy" Bray, sometimes known as the "dancing preacher" was unconventional in his methods, passionate in his quest to serve God and as a result witnessed many miracles. In his early years, before he accepted his calling, Billy was better known for his love of drink and questionable morals. One of the bridging moments between the character who inspires us to pursue God's prompting and his former self came when Billy acquired a copy of John Bunyan's Visions of Heaven and Hell. This writing provoked a deep response that led to him leaving his bed that night, finding Christ upon his knees, and committing his life to serving His loving Saviour.

There are varying opinions on who gave Billy this book. Some say his friends, others suggest it could have come from his wife's family or was left him by his deceased grandfather. Even in his journal, Billy has no idea who left it there – but someone did, someone whose name is not recorded in the history books, but whose action encouraged a life to discover Christ in a real and powerful way.

Our tendency to "grade" our achievements in life can place an unhealthy importance or seeming unimportance on the things we do and share with others. We tend to think of someone sharing the Gospel publicly, with great passion, as being something much more important than baking a cake for an elderly neighbour –

or passing a book onto someone. The returning missionary who has amazing stories of dramatic conversions can seem much more "used of God" than the humble person who regularly sits and listens to work colleagues who need some support. This unknown character in the life of Billy Bray helps us see such acts in a new light. God's glory can rest on the simplest of life's interactions, regardless of whether we view them as "spiritual" or not.

There is great worth in what some would term the mundane routines of life: those daily jobs, conversations, work habits and us just "getting on" with things. But the landscape of such interactions and relationships can carry the colours of His life. They declare God's creative majesty and what we see is just a fraction of the wider picture being shaped by His ever-loving Hand. From the words of a powerful sermon to the act of leaving a book for someone to read, the fragrance of a worshipful life is ever present. You just have to breathe it in.

Moments to reflect

"How priceless is your unfailing love!
Both high and low among men find a refuge in the shadow of your wings.
They feast on the abundance of your house;
you give them drink from your river of delights.
For with you is the fountain of life;
in your light we see light."

(Psalms 36:7-9 NIV)

"I thank God that the kingdom of God is not divided
into areas for big,
important people and areas for little, unimportant people.
Every one is just as needful in God's sight as any other!"

A. W. Tozer, Why We Must Think Rightly About God

Prayer:

"Lord, Your heart towards me is priceless, like a banner held above my head, speaking of Your mercy and compassion. I want so deeply to get caught up in the fury of Your love, living a life that is convinced beyond any shadow of doubt of my worth and value in Your sight – the apple of Your eye. Let my actions towards others be an expression of this love. Let Your fragrance permeate my every decision, thought, word and action."

9: The Fragrance of a Surrendered Life

"All to Jesus I surrender;
All to Him I freely give.
I will ever love and trust Him,
In His presence daily live.
I surrender all, I surrender all.
All to Thee, my blessed Saviour. I surrender all."

I Surrender All by Judson W. Van DeVenter, 1896

A life surrendered to the will of God has a beautiful fragrance to it – a perfume carried by the wind of His Spirit, that dances and sways on the current of His breeze. The attention of the casual "passer-by" is arrested by such a person as they catch a sense of the aroma. They look from side to side, up and down, all around, to try and find the origins of such a scent – yet their frantic survey finds no person. Instead, they are left there standing in a melee of questions, leading them to contemplate an inner search of the deepest part of their heart. Sometimes the best questions are those that lead to more questions.

The bouquet can be found in many places, never restricted to one location. Sometimes one can catch its scent between the pages of The Foxes Book of Martyrs, sometimes in the simple testimony and activity pages of a congregational newsletter. Maybe it is even sensed during a visit to a local supermarket, classroom or at an evening dinner party with friends.

The wind of the Spirit seems to find all the nooks and crannies of our daily life, bringing with it little promptings of deeper things that are set out before us – a landscaped life shaped by our relationship with Christ, and of following Him into glorious and beautiful surrender. A life characterised by willingly choosing to embrace the cross of sacrifice that each pilgrim embodies.

For some, this cross will represent actions that are recorded in Martyrs' pages – to actually lay one's life down for the King. Most of us will never know such physical threats, but our cross still demands a valid and personally costly spiritual sacrifice. An invitation for the things that were once treasured, is humbly exchanged as we bow the knee at His Name and His throne. To continually see the re-prioritising of our lifestyle, we re-visit that constant question: "How far will I walk with this cross for my Saviour?"

Found within the September 1906 edition of The Apostolic Faith – a free newspaper and update service that came from the Azusa Street outpouring – is a small news paragraph about Brother Thos. Mahler. It reads: "A Pentecostal missionary has left for foreign lands, Bro' Thos. P. Mahler, a young man of German nationality. He has the gift of tongues besides the knowledge of several. He left here for San Bernardino. He may go by way of Alaska, Russia, Norway, Germany and to his destination in Africa. As our brother was leaving, Bro' Post spoke of his call and gave a message in tongues in regard to Bro' Mahler which he interpreted as follows: 'I have anointed this dear one with my Spirit, and he is a chosen vessel to me to preach the Gospel to many, and to suffer martyrdom in Africa.'"

This telling, yet small paragraph carries tones of a "laid-down" life – a life that followed a calling and dream to go and tell of a risen Christ. Sent out with prayers and blessings, the steps of this missionary were always moving toward his approaching death. Yet still he went.

The scent of sacrifice reaches the nostrils of heaven and hell in another story, this time a single mother who lives upon an estate in the outskirts of London. She has one teenage daughter who she is raising by herself, with no other family members nearby. Carrying the workload of keeping a flat, providing for her daughter and maintaining a part-time job, she balances her precarious hours with volunteering work at a support initiative for her community. She has no real time for herself and all her energy and income is willingly spent on her daughter or those who share the same air but deeper problems. A few miles away is another project, highly funded and more adept at promoting its work. If she moved location to work here she would surely be under less pressure, but she knows that the burden in her heart is for THIS estate, with all its ups and downs. She continues to work out her calling, carrying the cross of her passion.

A surrendered life to Christ has no standard blueprint, except that of His cross. The fruit of its embrace comes in many diverse ways, both hidden and revealed. Splinters from the journey scar the hands and prayerful steps guide the feet in a pilgrimage so eloquently described by Mrs Elizabeth Prentiss, as "an apprenticeship at the throne of grace ."

Moments to reflect

". . . and anyone who does not take his cross and follow Me is not worthy of Me.
Whoever finds his life will lose it, and whoever loses his life for My sake will find it."

(Matthew 10:38-39 NIV)

"If Jesus Christ be God and died for me, then no sacrifice can be too great for me to make for Him."

C. T. STudd.

Prayer:

"Like natures' morning chorus and blossoming flowers in spring, a life of worshipful surrender holds such glorious sounds and smells. Lord, continually lead me to the cross, so that my wants and desires can find their rightful place. Help me to see my life in a different way, as each footprint made resembles Your close embrace. Help me in all my weaknesses, where my desire stretches further than my strength. As I follow Your leading anywhere, regardless of the path ahead, let this truth be held close: that I fully trust in You. Because no matter where I go, You are forever with me. Thank you Father."

10: Our Constant First Love

"This is the day the Lord has made;
let us rejoice and be glad in it."

(Psalm 118:24 NIV)

One of the earliest scriptures I learnt was Psalm 118:24. I repeated this verse many times as I grew up, enjoyed listening to Keith Green sing about it, and even carried a little bookmark with those words written over a picture of a rising sun. And while this verse continued to remain within my memory, over time, the excitement of what it meant started to fade. And if any rejoicing was being made, it was more likely over the goals I was achieving and the dreams that I carried, rather than the dawning of a brand new day.

Two moments brought the truth of this verse back to me. The first was a day out with my wonderful god-daughter. My wife and I had decided to take her to a local coffee shop for a cake. In my head the plan was simple. The shop was only a ten-minute walk, so we could have a drink and some food, then make our way over to the playground, giving us enough time to get home before it got dark. What I didn't realise was how our god-daughter saw the world around her. An hour and a half later we still had not arrived at the café. This precious little girl was finding so many wonderful pleasures in each flower and show of nature that we passed along the way that we just had to forget about the destination altogether!

The second moment came when I visited the village that saw the Hebrides Revival. I counted it a high privilege to be able to spend time with a few aging people who had lived through those rain drops from heaven. The place carried with it the history of being part of a wonderful visitation of the Lord's presence.

After a few conversations, I was given the opportunity to travel around the sites of history that had been so soaked in spiritual significance, each lovingly recorded. Each stop along the "tour" only strengthened the realisation within me that I was looking at something completely different to what my guide was seeing. While I was observing the buildings, broken ruins and pillars of stone, my companion was quietly content, caught up in a worshipful moment. Throughout the hours spent with him I discovered that while those structures that stirred my excitement still carried a personal worth of remembrance for him, his heart was captured upon something far more precious: the beauty of that day that His Lord had made.

Some of the most well known truths we have learnt over our years carry such wondrous wealth. Their words and phrases reveal precious aspects of our God, whose marvellous glory overshadows all of our greatest achievements. The stories we tell that can paint such powerful accounts of our works, both past and present, seem pale compared to joining in with just one note of praise from the heavenly hosts. These priceless truths lie deep within us, engraved in our hearts. Yet how easy it is for us to leave these familiar gems aside as we set our gaze upon the pursuit of the new to fill our ever-expanding vocabulary.

It is not about finding "old time" religion again, as this has nothing "old time" about it. Instead it's about the Alpha and Omega, the Beginning and the End, the Past, Present and Future. Even though time moves on and we grow up and learn countless new things, we must also remain captivated, forever enthralled by our first love.

From the elderly person who is brought to tears through the remembrance of lines in an ancient hymn to the young person who dances with enthusiasm to the latest contemporary song, the feeling of that first love captivates our senses, sweeps us into a deep embrace and never lets us go.

Oh what unspeakable joy it is to be caught up in His love! How wonderful it is to see His beauty and glory all around as we behold the tallest tree or the most delicate of flowers. To dance in the rain with such freedom, then stare at the night sky that displays His creative power. What an embrace we feel when we remember the cross, His great act of love that never diminishes – then cherishing His mercy that wraps around us, as we are brought to tears in humble brokenness.

No foundation is stronger than our first love – a state of being, a way of life that is constant, that is forever enthralled with His presence. Here, the familiar verses carry life like the very first time they were heard. The simplest of truths become the cornerstones of the life that we build upon, where the rhythm of our heart is not just about the end destination, but the treasuring of the wealth that is the journey – our journey of being in love with Him.

Moments to reflect

"The heavens declare the glory of God;
the skies proclaim the work of his hands.
Day after day they pour forth speech;
night after night they display knowledge.
There is no speech or language
where their voice is not heard.
Their voice goes out into all the earth,
their words to the ends of the world."

(Psalms 19:1-4 NIV)

"Religion to Billy was not a duty to be done,
not a privilege to be enjoyed in leisure hours,

not a benefit club, a comfortable provision for 'rainy days';
it was a life.
Never left behind, never put off with the Sunday's clothes,
never hidden before the great or low, good or bad.
But in him, flowing through him, speaking in every word,
felt in every action, seen in every look."

F.W. Bourne, Billy Bray, The King's Son

Prayer:

"Is there a more beautiful thing than this great dance of love, my Lord, where my heart is captivated by such a thought of You? My senses find furious energy as Your passion towards me is displayed so vividly all around me. Creation continually declares Your wonders, its speeches of love soaking deep into every detail of my life. Oh, to marinate in this joyous truth, this truth so real: that I am loved! May my life never become a familiar routine, where my walk with you is done without thought and passion. Instead, let my dance of love be like the breath I take, naturally done, but full of Your life-giving purpose."

11: Step Out With Both Feet

"While David was at Horesh in the Desert of Ziph, he learned that Saul had come out to take his life. And Saul's son Jonathan went to David at Horesh and helped him find strength in God. 'Don't be afraid,' he said. 'My Father Saul will not lay a hand on you. You will be king over Israel, and I will be second to you.'... Now the Philistines fought against Israel; the Israelites fled before them, and many fell slain on Mount Gilboa. The Philistines pressed hard after Saul and his sons, and then killed his son Jonathan."

(1 Samuel 23:15-17; 31:1-2 NIV)

Someone once told me about a minister. Here was a man who had embraced the calling upon his life to lead others towards the Lord. He rose up the spiritual ladder within his congregation and circle of projects, finding favour and success in many of the things he put his hands to. His career was looking good, a foundation laid for the latter years of his life. Then the tone of life changed as things started to crumble around this successful man. What once was a life that was considered strong, now had the definite cracks of human frailty appearing. Victorious moments were replaced with seemingly insurmountable obstacles.

A ministry that once ran with the stamina of the Spirit, now demanded an ever-increasing investment of personal energy. It burnt him out. And what was considered his greatest strength – his preaching – became his greatest weakness as his words started to dry up.

It didn't take long for me to realise that the man who shared this story with me was in fact describing himself. A man of God, who had seen many wondrous things, this storyteller had also experienced the pain of falling short. He smiled as he finished his tale. Speaking of the restoration and the joyous sermons he preached some years later, he finally figured out, through the mercy of His Saviour, what is now being recalled upon this page.

There is a character in the Bible called Jonathan. Best remembered for being the close friend of the future king, David, the first moment we hear of him he is a young fighter. Due to his conviction of the Lord's purpose, he fights the enemy while climbing up a hill as the rest of his army lies in fear. His action, and that of his armour bearer, raises the faith levels of his army and they join in with the fight. He is a brave warrior, a believer in his Lord, and someone who runs after the goal that is set before him.

A friendship is built between Jonathan and David, while his father, the king, watches on with jealousy and fear. All of them know that David will be king one day, and there comes a time when the three cannot remain together. David runs off, fearing for his life while Jonathan decides to stay with his father. A touching moment is recorded in 1 Samuel 23 where Jonathan is able to meet up with David while he is still on the run. Jonathan's friendship helps David to strengthen himself in the Lord as he makes the sober statement: "You will be king over Israel, and I will be second to you." The next mention of Jonathan is that he gets killed on a hill while running away from the enemy he once fought against.

It's a sombre account of a life that ended upon a place that once represented such great victory. A far cry from that wild character that ran up a hill to face his enemy years earlier. The storyteller I met tied his own story and that of Jonathan together by alluding to a lifestyle change that is a challenge to us all. He first reflected upon whether Jonathan never joined his friend fully because he wanted to somehow be a bridge between the two; and then questioned that perhaps the lure of kingdom riches was just too much for that final sacrificial choice? And although he understood that he will never know the answer within this lifetime, he acknowledged the similarity found within his own personal story.

He became too comfortable in his walk of faith – able to soak up the past moments of victory and success, while living with the spoils of a blessed life. Eventually those blessings became the norm, the expectations he lived with. It became such a part of his life that when the moment came for him to consider losing it all and stepping out into the unknown, he buckled. His answer was to try and compromise. A foot placed upon the water, while also keeping one inside the boat, just in case. The result was that he got very wet, trying to please the two masters that his life was trying to balance between.

Years have passed, and whatever gains and successes lie around him, he now chooses to hold them lightly as his eyes are fixed upon something far higher. He continues to tell those around him of the gem of truth he discovered through his own painful journey and of the lesson he takes from the life of Jonathan – that sometimes we have decisions to make that require us to step out of our own comfort zone of blessings. Our abilities may say that we can continue in compromise, giving a sense of artificial safety. But no greater blessing can be found than the total trust of our God without holding anything back. This is a miracle amidst the mundane.

Moments to reflect

"But Jesus immediately said to them:
'Take courage. It is I. Don't be afraid.'
'Lord, if it's You,' Peter replied, 'tell me to come to You on the water.'
'Come,' He said.
Then Peter got down out of the boat, walked on the water and came toward Jesus.
But when he saw the wind, he was afraid and, beginning to sink,

cried out, 'Lord, save me!'
Immediately Jesus reached out His hand and caught him."

(Matthew 14:27-31 NIV)

"Father, let me dedicate, all this year to Thee.
In whatever worldly state Thou wilt have me be.
Not from sorrow, pain or care, freedom dare I claim.
This alone shall be my prayer, glorify Thy Name.

If in mercy Thou wilt spare joys that yet are mine.
If on life, serene and fair, brighter rays may shine.
Let my glad heart, while it sings, Thee in all proclaim.
And, whate'er the future brings, glorify Thy Name.

If Thou callest to the cross, and its shadow come.
Turning all my gain to loss, shrouding heart and home.
Let me think how Thy dear Son to His glory came.
And in deepest woe pray on, glorify Thy Name."

Father Let Me Dedicate, lyrics by Lawrence Tuttiett, 1864

Prayer:

"Father, this is a simple truth, yet one of such profound exchange: Thank you that as I offer up my life to You, You offer yours back to me. Help me to keep my eyes set upon You – to follow Your lead and Your outstretched Hand. No matter what You set before me, let my cry be, 'Glorify Your Name!' And if I start to cherish what will eventually fade, may Your grace gently move my gaze back to the beauty of worth found in You and Your plans for me alone."

12: A Beauty In Weakness

"Be not ashamed to be the servant of others for the love of Jesus Christ, and to be reckoned poor in this life. Rest not upon yourself, but build your hope in God. Do what lies in your power, and God will help your good intent. Trust not in your learning, nor in the cleverness of any that lives, but rather trust in the favour of God, who resists the proud and gives grace to the humble."

Thomas a Kempis, The Imitation Of Christ, Ch4

Reverend James Harcourt was a talented man. "A rousing preacher, and an earnest labourer for souls." Asked by Potto Brown in 1844 to oversee the work in Houghton, Huntingdon, his preaching started to see a number of conversions and an increase of people to their chapel. This work started to extend into the neighbouring villages, but Potto was still searching for something more.

Brother Brown, as he was known by some, was a successful businessman, turned philanthropist. Originally a Quaker, then Congregationalist in 1837, he set about investing his time and finances into charitable and religious work, including the founding of the Houghton Chapel in 1840 with his business partner, Joseph Goodman. He had a keen interest to see the Gospel preached to all, yet was deeply stirred towards the part of the social class system of the day that he belonged to. So while he found joy in the good work of what this talented preacher was achieving, he also observed that his sermons were mainly reaching the poor and lower class. He so longed to see the Gospel impact further, including the salvation of his friend and business partner Goodman – and Reverend Harcourt saw that.

In the height of his success this preacher was also able to see his shortcomings, telling Brother Brown that, "something else must be done or he did not see that this class of persons would be reached at all." His suggestion (he had followed the lectures on revival by Charles G. Finney) was to propose that they invite him over to the UK. Brother Brown did just that, and Finney's impact in this country is still felt to this day.

The determination to fulfil all that He has laid within us, our talents and abilities that have been God-breathed inside us, carry such a powerful force. They are tough and withstand so much of life's temptations. They can break through obstacles and push us forward. Through commitment and passion we can achieve so much, standing upon that hill of accomplishment and staring upon the results of our efforts.

At times, weakness can seem to go against the grain of how we wish to walk. Yet there is great strength found within it, a strength only embraced when we humbly acknowledge its existence. It doesn't come from a stance of shame or a sense of failure, but a wise heart aware that we can't achieve any godly dream on our own. We are all creatures of such ability and potential, but only, somehow, when we embrace those things we lack. Instead of shared weakness being a sign of feebleness or impotence, our wonderful Saviour uses our vulnerability as fertile ground for His strength to be truly sown and grown.

This odd acceptance – that it is okay to be far from strong in all things – does not seem to always make human sense. In this pilgrimage we will have days of great rejoicing as we come rushing back to our Saviour saying, "even the demons submit to us in Your name." Then we find we have moments when we can't even stay up with our Lord in His time of sorrow. There are days when we see the wondrous works of our Christ and days where we fear for our lives in a storm-hit boat; moments when our ideas impact our local community and moments where the next project we try falls flat on its face.

In this balance of our strengths and weaknesses we see a wonderful treasure embodied: Him! – covering us with His wings of mercy, providing a warmth that gives us a different type of strength; a strength that balances out our life, that of our frailty and trophies of achievements. That is why we can say, "In our weakness He is strong," because of Him, and Him alone.

Moments to reflect

"But He said to me,
My grace is sufficient for you,
for My power is made perfect in your weakness.
Therefore I will boast all the more gladly about my weaknesses,
so that Christ's power may rest upon me.
That is why, for Christ's sake, I delight in weaknesses,
in insults, in hardships, in persecutions, in difficulties.
For when I am weak, then I am strong."

(2 Corinthians 12:9-10 NIV)

"When you love you walk on water.
Just don't stumble on the waves.
We all want to go there somethin' awful.
But to stand there it takes some grace . . .
We are frail, we are fearfully and wonderfully made.
Forged in the fires of human passion.
Choking on the fumes of selfish rage.
And with these our hells and our heavens so few inches apart.
We must be awfully small.
And not as strong as we think we are."

We Are Not as Strong as We Think We Are by Rich Mullins
Reunion © 1996

Prayer:

"A gentle comforting peace surrounds my soul each time I reflect upon my care within Your hands. No matter if I display strength or feet of clay, You hold me close in a merciful embrace. Let my heart cry out, "I am strong in You, not from my skills but from the truth that I am loved!" So help me not run away from the signs of my humanity, but to see the beauty of this life in all its highs and lows. To be a pilgrim of the cross, which is so dear within my heart, is to travel in humble acknowledgment that I need You more each day. This is your design and desire for me. Thank you Father. "

13: The Strength of Less

"'You are old, father William,' the young man said, 'and your hair has become very white; and yet you incessantly stand on your head – do you think, at your age, it is right?'"

Lewis Carroll, Alice's Adventures in Wonderland

Personal strength is a challenging concept in our faith. As the famous quote goes, "Surely any old dead fish can float down the river, but it takes one with a backbone to swim against the tide." There are many self-help books, rules and guidelines for sale about what can build up our "inner spirit". There is even a large range of opinions around concerning what makes someone a "good" and "productive" Christian. I guess all of us would desire to grow stronger in our faith; to be men and women who don't "go with the flow" and whim of others' belief systems, but allow ourselves to swim upstream in our pursuit of godly passions.

The story of Gladys Aylward is well known from the 1958 film The Inn of the Sixth Happiness, and from her limited but enlightening personal writings. Born in London in 1902, she lived a life of quiet domestic service. After reading stories of desperate need from the "Young Life Campaign" material, she felt a call to become a missionary to China. Applying to a mission society in the hope of finding an avenue for her calling, she found that she was turned down due to her age, lack of experience and education.

Her reactions to the disappointment show her maturity and willingness to learn. Following on from the Mission Society Board's rejection after her three months at the missionary college, she replied, "I'm sorry I can't be one of your missionaries, but God knows best. I haven't learned much at the college, it wouldn't go in, somehow; but I have learned to pray, and that's something I never knew, and something I'll always be thankful for."

The board then offered her the role of housekeeper in Bristol for two of their retired missionaries who were too old to look after themselves. The acceptance led to her seeing and experiencing a side of faith that would shape and train her. "She had heard of such faith, but she had never met anybody who trusted in God so utterly and implicitly. She joined in their family prayers and, bit by bit, she saw that they knew God as their own friend, and that they lived with Him." They told her stories of their life overseas: "God never lets you down. He sends you, He guides you, and He provides for you. He may not answer your prayer as you think He will, but He answers it. He has always answered our prayers." The old missionaries helped her wait, to be patient, and to trust God.

It wasn't long before she did find her way to China, providing support for Mrs Jeannie Lawson who was a missionary there. Eventually taking over this work, she became well-known in particular for the perilous journey she undertook to lead two groups of children to safety from the Japanese invasion of 1938.

The journey for a follower of Christ moves us down many roads as we embody the great and sure hope. Yet, within its many routes, there lies a common path – the way of the cross. A continued embrace and growing recognition of its role within our lives makes us both weaker and stronger at the same time. An act of worship that is above any words or visual presentations, the path of the cross is a beautiful symphony of the God who we love. In precious moments of devotion and trust, those selfless words emerge, "Not my will, but yours be done."

Defying gender and healing the past, the cross lays aside qualifications and breaks the "norm". The old dare to stand upon their heads with energy and vigour whilst the young confound the scholars with wisdom beyond their years. A domestic servant can ignore the odds and preach the Gospel of Christ to China, and people like you and me can journey the impossible road due to His guiding Hand.

This is the backbone within us, the backbone of the strength of less. Less of us and more of Him.

Moments to reflect

"Sacrifice and offering you did not desire,
but my ears you have pierced,
burnt offerings and sin offerings you did not require.
Then I said
Here I am, I have come,
it is written about me in the scroll.
I desire to do your will, O my God;
your law is within my heart."

(Psalms 40:6-8 NIV)

"There are hidden treasures,
wrought in the darkness of dawn
and the heat of the noon on the anvil of experience,
and beaten into wondrous form by the mighty stroke of the divine."

Jim Cymbala, Complete works of E.M. Bounds
(Baker Books, 2004)

Prayer:

"My God who is above all things, yet also chooses to become a servant, it is such a cherished privilege to be a pilgrim of Your cross. Within this great act of Your love, I find freedom and hope without measure. Thank you for the truth of knowing that all my works and high stature amount to nothing in comparison to the sound of Your heartbeat and feeling You near. May the frequent temptation to strive in my own strength find no foundation within my life, as I continually seek my home within the secret and quiet place. May my will be entwined with yours as you shape my life on Your potter's wheel, moulding me into the shape that most resembles the risen Christ."

14: A Co-Operating Disciple

"Simon Peter and another disciple were following Jesus. Because this disciple was known to the high priest, he went with Jesus into the high priest's courtyard, but Peter had to wait outside at the door. The other disciple came back, spoke to the girl on duty there and brought Peter in."

(John 18:15-17 NIV)

Reverend G.R. Harding Wood expressed it so wonderfully in the foreword to his 1952 book, A Year with Our Lord: Sunday School Lessons, when he wrote: "I am writing this Foreword in the form of a letter, and I hope that you will look upon it as a personal message to you as a co-operator with me in this attempt to teach boys and girls the Good News of the Lord Jesus."

To be a Co-operator, acting jointly and collaborating with Christ is such a wonderful privilege and goal for our lives. There is a beauty that confounds the most eloquent of social theories and political ideals: that each person carries a worth and importance that is intrinsically linked to others. In the outworking of our Lord's purpose, He has created an evolving masterpiece of art that not only calls upon us all to value each other, but lays before us a most staggering revelation on how He walks with us in the background scenes of life that no one else notices.

The story of Simon Peter during the betrayal, death and resurrection of our Lord is a dramatic one. From the self belief that he would never turn his back upon his Master, to the impacting moment of being told that before the cock crowed he would do just that, makes us hold our breath. We see the raw emotion of him facing his darkest night, denying his friend three times as he sits by a charcoal fire. He then catches a glimpse of Jesus and we sense the weight of his oaths start to dawn upon him. Running away in failure, then being sought out and welcomed by his resurrected Saviour, he sits again by a charcoal fire, a fire that must have brought memories back for both men. This most staggering of storylines that holds both our heart and emotions captive, finishes with Peter standing boldly on that day of Pentecost, explaining with clarity and conviction the out-breaking of the Spirit of God.

Two characters seem initially prominent within this narrative, that of our Lord Jesus Christ and His disciple, Peter. But interwoven within the tapestry of this journey is another individual – a character simply known as the "other disciple" – the person who knew the gatekeeper of the courtyard and was able to get the door open for Peter to walk into the unfolding storyline.

This simple act, performed by the unnamed disciple, carries with it such inspiring tones of encouragement. Their interaction was vital for the journey of Peter. Without this unnamed friend we would not be privy to the amazing fall and rise of Jesus' precious disciple. As the story stands, however, we can see the beautiful tale of their lives braided together.

One look around our congregations, communities, families and friendship groups, reveals tones of contributions that hidden lives have played within the wider composition of God's purpose. Lives of quiet distinctiveness that have become blended with a wider story – many individual contributions missed by earthly eyes. Yet there is a Father watching.

This knowledge takes us beyond the demand of applause or praise from those around and sets our gaze upon being content with faithfully worshiping our Saviour through our walk in life – a walk that acknowledges both the days of receiving high acclaim and the moments of being unknown; but both finding their position in the attitude of devotion to the One we love and adore.

And it is here, at this worshipful place, that we find that our lives carry such great wealth; contributions to endless story lines that are being outplayed. From the smallest to the largest interaction, we witness an unshakable reality – that our life's breath holds a priceless significance for not only this day, but for the days to come. And when it comes to any recognition, nothing surpasses the embrace of our Saviour as His Words declare over us, "Well done my good and faithful friend."

Moments to reflect

"I have fought the good fight, I have finished the race,
I have kept the faith.
Now there is in store for me the crown of righteousness,
which the Lord, the righteous Judge, will award to me on that day –
and not only to me, but also to all who have longed for His appearing."

(2 Timothy 4:7-8 NIV)

"Search all my thoughts, the secret springs,
The motives that control;
The chambers where polluted things hold empire o'er the soul.
Thus prostrate I shall learn of thee, what now I feebly prove;
That God alone in Christ can be, unutterable love."

Unutterable Love by Francis Bottome (1823-1894)

Prayer:

"Search me, O Lord, and mould my life to walk with steps that worship You. Leaving the pursuit of earthly praise, and pressing forward to finish this race, help me value the life I have, seeing worth in all that I contribute and give. May these actions be an echo of my worship as my life displays my relationship with You. I am continually in awe and wonder of this truth, that You invite me to collaborate in this unfolding story of Love. So let this prayer remain on my lips, 'Help me keep this faith until I hear Your words said over me, "Well done!"'"

15: The Paradox of Love

"To have found God and still to pursue Him is the soul's paradox of love, scorned indeed by the too-easily-satisfied religionist, but justified in happy experience by the children of the burning heart."

A. W. Tozer, Pursuit of God

Harold Lawrence Cuthbert Horton was born in Wrexham, North Wales in 1881. A Pentecostal pastor and author, he lived during the time of a movement that focused heavily on faith and belief in the Holy Spirit, filled with well-known devotees such as Howard Carter, Smith Wigglesworth and the Jeffreys brothers.

His name may not be well-known when compared to such characters, and his exploits may not be recorded in many books, yet Harold's life carried a wonderful beauty and gifting from God that wove itself into this sometimes chaotic period. New and rediscovered doctrines, challenges around perceptions, and struggles with existing journeys of exploration were all part and parcel of this chapter in history. It was a time of upheaval, but also a time of holding onto the core essence of faith and doctrine. Many influential figures were on a journey of re-imagination and discovery that also brought the temptation of division, arrogance and misunderstanding. And amidst this turbulence, journeyed Harold.

He was a man who gave up his professorship in a university to teach in a Bible college. He spent his time writing up the debates, the sermons and the material that some of the people of this time were speaking of, capturing the conversations, questions and inner battles that were spreading through the dialogues. Then diligently, Harold transformed those rough notes and disjointed explorations into a readable form for people to truly digest.

These notes were not just legible words on a page, but sentences and outlines that captured the turmoil, the prayers and sleepless nights of struggle that each of those worshipers of Christ grappled with. From the visually prominent to the hidden traveller on the back row of the congregation, Harold was able to hear the beat of their heart and the complexity of their words. Valuing each persons' journey, Harold was ever-mindful of trying to find ways in which distant conversations could be heard by all.

Our walk of faith and service can be full of excitement. Our steps are made, not only as an individual, but as part of a congregation and community, and provide momentum and purpose within our spiritual life. Yet this walk of intimacy and truth that we treasure so dearly, is also one of openness and learning, which A.W. Tozer seems to capture so perfectly with the paradox of love: of finding God and yet still pursuing Him.

This journey of worship and of resting within His arms displays the parallel truths that God walks besides us, but is also holding us in the palm of His hand. That mixture of closeness and vastness, of leaning on His chest and hearing His heartbeat, yet also marvelling at the universe and trembling in awe of His Holy presence, needs holding in delicate and intentional balance.

To some, this may seem a contradiction, but to those who have run towards His cry whilst being sure of His presence, these two parts of knowing Christ are in complete harmony. The pursuit of Him is part of His invitation for us to truly see and understand the world around us. He is not constricted to one sermon, one insight, or one image. He is everywhere, revealing His nature through creation so perfect and vast and His love through human vessels so imperfect and small.

The life of Harold serves as a gentle reminder that our journey of discovery is one of intimacy with God – both for whole individuals and whole nations. But that intimacy also has a twist. The singular and corporate does not just relate to our favourite groupings, books or latest sermons, even though they are worthy of our notice. It asks us to consider listening to those outside our normal circles; to lay our prejudice, misconceptions, and arguments to one side and gaze upon the weight of the cross. This goes beyond any disagreement, conclusion and interpretation, and centres upon our pursuit of Him alone.

This is truly a paradox of love: that to intimately discover Him also requires walking in worshipful unity and intimacy with those who mimic Him – our fellow pilgrims.

Moments to reflect

"And I pray that you, being rooted and established in love,
may have power, together with all the saints,
to grasp how wide and long and high and deep
is the love of Christ,
and to know this love that surpasses knowledge –
that you may be filled to the measure of all the fullness of God.
Now to Him who is able to do immeasurable
more than all we ask or imagine,
according to His power that is at work within us,
to Him be glory in the church and in
Christ Jesus throughout all generations,
for ever and ever! Amen."

(Ephesians 3:17-21 NIV)

"The growth of grace is like the polishing of metals.
There is first an opaque surface;
by and by you see a spark darting out, then a strong light;

till at length it sends back a perfect image of the sun that shines upon it."

Edward Payson, Congregational Preacher (1783-1827),
The works of Edward Payson

Prayer:

"To be continually captured by the discovery of You, is my humble prayer, O Lord. Help me never to sit upon a high perch of gathered knowledge and look down on any brother or sister, but to allow the wealth of Your love to soften my heart, the way only Your merciful touch can. Teach me to celebrate the grace that is active in all our lives, and see Your image in every face. Help me to treat those around me with a constant, ever-replenished love and see the marks of the cross on my fellow travellers in this life. Remind me daily that the scars of Your love put my minuscule disagreements and arrogant assertions in their place."

16: The Moment

"Guard well your spare moments. They are like uncut
diamonds. Discard them and their value will never
be known. Improve them and they will become
the brightest gems in a useful life."

Ralph Waldo Emerson

"Moments" are important – uncut diamonds that carry such
a wealth of life, but are only truly discovered when we recognise
them for what they are.

In 1765, Granville Sharp visited his brother, William, who
was the King's Surgeon, but who also regularly ran a local surgery
for the poor in Mincing Lane, London. That evening, Granville was
confronted with a black slave called Jonathan Strong. He had
been severely beaten and flogged by his master then discarded in
the street. There was very little remaining of the left side of his
face and he was in desperate need of some medical attention.
Granville and his brother attended to his injuries then took him
to a hospital, where they covered the bill for his four-month stay.
Once Jonathan recovered from his injuries, the Sharp brothers
found employment for him.

Two years later, Jonathan's old master tracked him down and
tried to kidnap him with the aim of selling him on. This ultimately
led to a court case where Granville, realising that the English
law favoured the right of the master, fought for the interpretation
of the law to favour liberty for all. The case was eventually won.
Jonathan was a free man, who lived in England for five years
until he died from his past injuries.

That moment in time, an evening's visit to his brothers surgery,
revealed the wealth of this uncut diamond. His decision to act

dramatically changed the direction of his efforts in this world. The path he chose didn't just impact the life of Jonathan Strong, but led Granville on a journey where he would confront the very issues of the abolition of slavery. In later years, when others would press forward with this grassroots campaign, Granville Sharp became known by many as the "Grand Old Man" of the abolition movement.

To have purposes, dreams and passions are such wonderful aspects of our created being, part of the marvellous fingerprint of life that we all carry. They provide momentum for us, an unseen energy that pushes us forward, while giving substance and meaning to what we choose to put our hands towards. It is a joyous statement to shout out, "I will press forward and take hold of all that God has for me!"

Our desire to get from "a" to "b" can provide us with such strength and commitment, but our speed through life can also lead us to miss the most beautiful of landscapes that pass us by.

We could initially think that the answer should be that we slow down and widen our tunnel vision. Yet the rough edges of this diamond seem to hint at something different. It doesn't point towards a schedule or a plan that we follow. Neither does it inform the speed of travel, as there is no conformity to what tempo we should set. Instead, as it bypasses our desire for rules and outlines, it focuses our attention upon something far more challenging: the moment.

To embrace the moment we must be willing to be led. We must carefully grasp the responsibility of what God has placed within us, but lay it down at His feet. Sometimes the gifts that we hold so dear only find their full voice in sacrifice, as they are led by His prompting and our worshipping heart to be given over wholly to Him.

Granville Sharp was a wonderful musician. Many may have assumed that his destiny lay in the world of music, but the moment he helped Jonathan his journey took on a different expression. The Lord of freedom led him to speak up for those who were unheard – to learn, interpret and defend the law of the land until those imprisoned were free. His ability and gifting provided many spaces for his music to be heard, while also gathering support for the cause of the abolition movement.

It can be a hard thing to hold our gifting and purpose loosely in this way. Yet the gentle hand of our Saviour encourages us to let go of our own control and, in turn, trust Him with what He has placed within us. When our starting point is not about personal fulfilment and the achievement of our goals, but about the wonderful relationship of loving Him and our neighbour, there is overwhelming blessing. We must seek to be flexible enough to journey where that moment of relationship leads, and to be at peace knowing that we are enfolded in His wings.

Moments to reflect

"So don't be so surprised when I tell you
that you have to be 'born from above' – out of this world, so to speak.
You know well enough how the wind blows this way and that.
You hear it rustling through the tree,
but you have no idea where it comes from or where it's headed next.
That's the way it is with everyone 'born from above'
by the wind of God, the Spirit of God."

(John 3:7-8 The Message)

"So breathe it in and breathe it out.
Listen to your heartbeat.
There's a wonder in the here and now.

It's right there in front of you.
And I don't want you to miss the miracle of the moment."

Miracle of the Moment by Steven Curtis Chapman
Sparrow © 2007

Prayer:

"My God, the creator of the universe, You sing over us with such pleasure and joy. I pray that I never remain static, but move within this great dance of life that You are outworking. Fill me with an understanding of how to balance the investment I must give with what You stir up in my heart. Help me never to ignore the beauty of Your prompting. I know my sight is so limited, but You Lord know the beginning from the end. So today, in this precious and unrepeated moment, I lay down my hopes and dreams and declare that You are in control. What beautiful peace surrounds me in the certainty that all my desires and longings in the present, and all I hope for the future, are in Your care."

17: The Balance

"Stop helping God across the road
like a little old lady."

Stand Up Comedy by U2
(© 2009 Universal-Island Records Ltd)

It is such a mystery to dwell upon our relationship with God, to remember that the Creator of the universe, whose hand has shaped the most awe-inspiring beauty, has also breathed life so intimately into our mouths. His breath kisses our lives and resides within us in an unapproachable, yet approachable, holiness. His presence brings us to the floor in devotional worship, allowing us moments of reflection and repositioning. The 1912 hymn In the Garden puts it thus:

"He walks with me,
and He talks with me,
And He tells me I am His own.
And the joy we share as we tarry there,
None other has ever known."

This scale of opposites defies our clever logic. The beautiful enigma is that God's ways are boundless, higher, greater and unfathomable and yet He chooses and even longs to be known, understood and loved. Is it any wonder we each desire the very same? This heavenly truth is our soul's destiny as well as its delight. So why is it that whilst we occasionally sense our need of the heavy weight of our Father's presence, often we content ourselves with a distant snatched glimpse of His throne room?

We pitch our tent in the knowledge of His favour, but not in the shared intimacy of His friendship. We focus on our inheritance as His children rather than on our relationship with our Father.

We sing more about our feelings, than about His faithfulness. We lose sight of what should be our only view. Starting to think that the hills to be overcome can be conquered in our own strength, and imposing our desires through our prayers, we fake asking God for His will to be done, when we have preferred our own.

In 2001 I came across a group of people who got together each month to pray for a particular ministry. This organisation had been around for many years, and had faithfully served countless people. Its list of projects had brought great admiration in many circles around the world, but had recently struggled with some significant practical changes.

I was invited to come along to one of their prayer meetings, so I sat at the back and observed those who had congregated. The majority were elderly women, quietly spoken with a humble sense of dignity shining from them. Afterwards, over tea and cake, I heard how, for over forty years, they had faithfully gathered and prayed. They had seen this ministry rise in heights of recognition and also walked in the valleys of challenge and opposition. Business plans and product launches had come and gone over that time, with many updates and new ideas that needed their prayerful support.

They had seen it all – praise reports and prayer alerts – and in it all they remained firm in their belief. There was a sense of peace in their words and outlook upon life, which went past the hopes that were written upon the latest bulletin that was sent their way. Life's lines upon their faces revealed years of existence that had been spent within a prayerful space – one that could not be taught with words or lesson plans, only experienced upon bended knees. They had a gentle contentment that this ministry was the Lord's work. And while it required careful, practical management, the overseer was God. He was in control, and its end or flourishing would only come from Him.

It can be easy for us to default into rising up, standing in our own strength, to "fight the good fight". Maybe a crisis dawns before us, or a great idea that could spark some positive momentum happens within our life or community. Yet within all the available options open to us, this aging prayer group shows something that seems so simple yet profound: that for us to run or stand, we must learn to stop and sit. To paraphrase Watchman Nee, "In order to stand in the armour of God, we must first learn to sit and walk with Him."

To sit in His presence is not a static thing. Sitting is sometimes harder than moving. Sitting moulds our priorities and in turn, balances out our outlook upon life. Sitting speaks of a submission and a life powered by the reality of His strength. As we deliberately lean our ear towards His whispering voice or fall prostrate at His bellowing tone, we sense His holiness. We have the stability that we are loved by God, cherished and highly adored. But we are also worshippers of the Almighty God of the heavens and of earth.

What peace and comfort resides in the beautiful knowledge that we can live within that balance – a balance that goes beyond explanation, but is found in trusting worship to Him – bringing a steadiness to our walk where we honour our gifting and abilities, but also seeing that no helping hand from us can help God cross the road; a road He created Himself.

Moments to reflect

"The heavens praise Your wonders, O Lord,
Your faithfulness too, in the assemble of the holy ones.
For who in the skies above can compare with the Lord?
Who is like the Lord among the heavenly beings?
In the council of the holy ones God is greatly feared'
He is more awesome than all who surround Him.
O Lord God Almighty, who is like You?
You are mighty, O Lord, and Your faithfulness surrounds You."

(Psalm 89:5-8 NIV)

"O Lord my God, when I in awesome wonder.
Consider all, the works Thy Hand hath made.
I see the stars, I hear the mighty thunder.
Thy power throughout, the universe displayed.
Then sings my soul,
My Saviour, God to Thee.
How great Thou art, how great Thou art!"
How Great Thou Art!"

Lyrics Carol Boberg. English translation, Stuart K. Hine.

Prayer:

"I stand in awe of Your mighty Hand, revealed in creation so vast. I bow before Your Holy throne, in reverent worship and deep love. Allow me to walk in the knowledge of Your acceptance, but never to take for granted such astounding favour; to live a life that's unshakable and full of hope, but also to be perfectly content as I sit with You. Laying all my strength at the foot of the cross, embracing Your Life that flows deep within my veins. This, Oh Lord, is my simple prayer: let me trust You in humility in all my steps. Amen."

18: The Precious Oil of Unity

"Cannon to right of them,
Cannon to left of them,
Cannon in front of them, volleyed and thundered;
Stormed at with shot and shell,
Boldly they rode and well,
Into the jaws of death,
Into the mouth of Hell, rode the six hundred."

Alfred Tennyson, Charge of the Light Brigade

The 25th October 1854 saw the charge of the Light Brigade during the Battle of Balaclava. It was a famous and heartfelt episode in the history of the Crimean War that saw lives lost and nations impacted. Each moment within that account is fascinating, but I wish to focus upon one stroke within time's clock face. Come with me to a disagreement that happened a few years earlier in 1847, and which caused an avalanche of different decisive actions.

Palestine was under the control of the Turkish Empire, but the Church of the Nativity was given over jointly to both Greek Orthodox and Roman Catholic monks. A squabble developed between these two groups due to the Orthodox monks removing a star from the spot in which the Catholics believed once stood the revered manger. This later turned into a small battle where lives were lost, as both sides refused to back down. In 1852 this escalated even more, with the Catholic monks placing the star back upon their holy spot. Again, this disagreement between the two factions led to the cost of lives and tensions running high. The Orthodox monks asked for help from Tsar Nicholas of Russia, who then proceeded to show his protection with a number of self-interested actions, one of them being to attack the Turkish Empire. Britain, fearing the implications of that attack, then defended the Turkish Empire by attacking Russia. Thus leading the nations into the Crimean War.

There are, of course, many other reasons that contributed to that horrendous period of history, but this story must cause us to consider how our personal actions can have far-reaching implications. Our passionate arguments that seem desperately important to us can lead to the building of opposing camps, where we, as an individual or within a group, can find our identity in a set of rules and opinions, rather than in the Holy Cornerstone Himself.

For two years I was able to spend time with a gentle Catholic man called Damian. Our first encounter was not the easiest, as it seemed to revolve around my personal quest to convince him that my own interpretation of Scripture was the correct one to pursue. It wasn't a dialogue, more a monologue, as he just sat quietly as I rambled on. At the end of my passionate speech, he smiled and then asked if he could have the privilege of praying with me. My immediate response was "Yes!" I thought that his comment was an indication of his turning towards my point of view. Yet as we prayed, I realised that this privilege was less about my determined points, and more about the wonderful truth that we both loved Jesus.

Over those few years I saw how this precious man's life was able to walk humbly around arguments and opinions, while stretching forth his arms in a loving embrace. It wasn't a dismissal of a position, but simply an acknowledgment that if we were to truly hear about each persons' glimpse of their Saviour, we must first set our eyes upon our common chord of love. It is here that we see each other in a different light; it is here, that we truly believe that each one of us has a value that we honour. Our interpretations and out-workings may be diverse, and someone's theological standpoint may be far from our own, but we all add tone to this beautiful chorus of worship that rises towards Him.

Our Saviour makes a beautiful statement that also attaches with it a great challenge to our own walk: "Let me give you a new command: Love one another. In the same way I loved you, you love one another. This is how everyone will recognize that you are my disciples—when they see the love you have for each other" (John 13:34-35 The Message). Love has a way of avoiding being used if all we are about is amplifying our own viewpoints. Love moves past our soapboxes and leads our heart to Christ's greatness. It is here that all knees bow down and high opinions humble themselves, as His gentle leading shows us the hope of brothers and sisters dwelling in unity.

It is a hope that is not far away or too high upon a mountain to grasp. It's not hidden deep in some far-off jungle or only attained by a perilous voyage. It is a hope that is before our eyes, sitting next to us in our pew and also across the street in another church building. No matter the activity or the invitation list that is made, hope is ever present.

Why? Because this hope is found in each one of us! A hope that shines out as we stretch out our hands in love to one another in a precious tie of unity. It rings out in such beautiful tones that its foundation stone is not some meeting or agreed theological statement, but open palms lifted up in worship, as His precious oil is poured upon those who dwell together in harmony.

Moments to reflect

"How good and pleasant it is
when brothers live together in unity!
It is like precious oil poured on the head,
running down on the beard,
running down on Aaron's beard

down upon the collar of his robes.
It is as if the dew of Hermon
were falling on Mount Zion.
For there the Lord bestows his blessing,
even life forevermore."

(Psalm 133:1-3 NIV)

"I think if we were given the Scriptures,
it was not that we could prove that we were right about everything.
If we were given the Scriptures,
it was to humble us into realizing that God is right
and the rest of us are just guessing."

Homeless Man by Rich Mullins
Reunion © 2003

Prayer:

"My precious Lord, may my heart be continually captivated by this hope of unity. Let my brothers and sisters lift up their hands in unified worship to You. Let my voice join in with this diverse tone of praise, as this spectrum of colour displays Your glory and life. May any misconception I have of those around me bow its knee before You. May my proud opinions find no soapbox as I lay all that I have at Your feet. Help me hold hands well with those who are holding on to Your hand too. Amen."

19: To Know Him

"Love never fails.
But where there are prophecies, they will cease;
where there are tongues, they will be stilled;
where there is knowledge, it will pass away.
For we know in part and we prophesy in part . . .
Now we see but a poor reflection as in a mirror;
then we shall see face to face.
Now I know in part;
then I shall know fully, even as I am fully known.
And now these three remain: faith, hope and love.
But the greatest of these is love."

(1 Corinthians 13:8-13 NIV)

Our journey of faith seems to invite us to be content in not seeing everything. To be those of simple faith where we don't know all the answers, we turn to the One who will point us in the right direction. It can be hard though, to be at peace in that state of flux, continually grasping something, only to find it opens up even more questions.

The world we live in seems to throw a curve ball at us, as it loudly promotes that answers are at our fingertips. One press of a keyboard and an ever-increasing giant encyclopaedia just appears right in front of our eyes. Documentaries that once just had a TV time slot, now have whole channels dedicated to our diverse craving for education. Laid out before us is a banquet of knowledge, bite-sized information chunks that can be easily digested as we speed through life.

There is something about our walk of faith that encourages us to breathe in each moment, inviting us to allow the steps of our pilgrimage and the lessons it brings, to mould and shape our lives. As we travel, we can experience a state of peace that is not dormant or lazy, but active and flexible upon the potters' wheel of life – where in our pursuit to learn and grow in our faith, we willingly slow down and rest with Him, placing into His hands what we know and have gathered through our diligent learning (along with that which we don't know and have gathered into a treasury of fear). And in worship with no regret, we begin to allow His moulding and reshaping work to reform our hearts and our minds. This is an ordinary miracle in itself.

This continual journey speaks of times where our outward appearance and walk is one of joy and visual fruit. Where fellow travellers passing by will see such blessings upon our life, as our labours produce such marvellous acts. But so preciously entwined within this walk, is also the moment of breaking and reshaping, as Saint John of the Cross so aptly describes as being our "dark night of the soul".

We all have times where our questions outweigh what we know, and the works of our hands that once produced such astounding things now carry more splinters than joyous satisfaction. Those who walk by may look upon our life and see the rawness of this time, assuming that our journey is off course or far from God. But this intimate occasion is not for an outward show, but a close and real embrace between our moulded life and His caring hands.

In His embrace, found both in our joys and tears, success and questions, an aroma of something precious rises through our being. Hints of something that will remain when all else fades away: faith, hope and love – and the greatest of these, love.

Found within our family and friendship groups, sitting next to us in our congregations and work offices, are lives that carry this precious jewel – love that has been fashioned through life's journey. Broken in pain and grief and polished in joy and happiness, their stories carry a depth that no one else can replicate, but all find a common strand in heaven's embrace. They live in that tension of not seeing in full, not having all the answers and not fully understanding all the paths they have taken, yet it is so perfectly balanced out with a peace that goes beyond all comprehension.

Like, for example, Deacon P of Camden, Deacon T of Rodman and Deacon B of Adams, whose lives were very briefly mentioned in R.A. Torrey's book, How To Pray. Along with these characters, "many others among the men and a large number of women" were consumed with Christ's love for themselves and for those around. From all backgrounds and ages, journeys of life and education, their experience of His precious love drew them upon a walk that many could not understand in full. Some onlookers and congregational members found these people's heart-cry for the salvation of the lost strange to digest. Some thought it showed an inner disturbance, which meant an illness or sickness approaching. And while their actions, time schedules and demonstrations of compassion could not be fully interpreted by many, the fruit of their lives could not be ignored. Their service and investment into their communities, both in prayer and practical support, paved the way for characters like Charles Finney and Reuben Torrey to recognise that the ground they stood upon had been tended by those who knew their God.

Moments to reflect

"Everything that goes into a life of pleasing God has been miraculously given to us
by getting to know, personally and intimately, the One who invited us to God.
So don't lose a minute in building on what you've been given,

complementing your basic faith with good character, spiritual understanding,
alert discipline, passionate patience, reverent wonder, warm friendliness, and generous love, each dimension fitting into and developing the others. With these qualities active and growing in your lives, no grass will grow under your feet,
no day will pass without its rewards as you mature in your experience of our Master Jesus."

(2 Peter 5:1-3; 5-8 The Message)

"I wanna believe, but I'm having a hard time seeing past
what I see right now, I see You right now.
I wanna be free, but when I try to fly I realise
I don't know how, no one showed me how.

I wanna believe when I close my eyes on this side
I'll wake up with You, more in love with You.
And finally You will say my race
It is over and my work is through? Cause I believed in You."

Help me believe by Kirk Franklin
Gospocentric © 2007

Prayer:

"My loving Father, whose treasures of life are immeasurable and never ending, may my sight broaden to see Your Hand upon my heart, as I soar freely in the heights as well as walk in the valleys below. Help me never to run from this indescribable embrace, seeing the worth of both my laughter and my tears. To be captivated by the discovery of You, growing as a disciple of love, this is my joy and my pain. This is my salvation and my suffering. Thank you Father that you humble but never humiliate and that you always lift my head as well as my heart."

20: Threads in His Story

"While women weep as they do now! I'll fight;
while little children go hungry as they do now, I'll fight;
while men go to prison, in and out, in and out,
as they do now; I'll fight –
I'll fight to the very end!"

William Booth, from The General Next To God
by Richard Collier

One of the famous images of William Booth is of him stumbling home, weary, clothes torn, with bandages around his head from stones that had been thrown at him. These were not one-off events, but would be part of the trials that his wife Catherine, the ever growing team, congregation, and himself would have to walk through as the work of the "Christian Mission" developed into the well known and highly respected mission of The Salvation Army.

Stories of bravery and commitment fill the annals of this work's history, with men and women of all ages and backgrounds, standing up for their faith and finding ways of demonstrating Christ's love to a hurting world; soldiers of the movement who outworked the three S's: "soup, soap and salvation" in many diverse ways. And as those years continued, the message of practical love and honouring our fellow brother and sister, spread into many different streams and avenues.

Two such avenues came prominently from the sons of William and Catherine Booth, and George and Marianne Railton (second in command of the Salvation Army). Bramwell Booth, working alongside a number of other figures, helped to publicise the issue of child prostitution within the country, eventually seeing the age of consent rise to sixteen through the 1885 Criminal Law Amendment Act. The Reverend David Railton, a Church of England clergyman, helped establish The Tomb of the Unknown Soldier that still enables us to remember those who have fallen.

The life and work of these early founders plays out a wonderful tone of faith that we are all to hear. The raw message of the Gospel life that it declared so clearly, that practical love and compassion, walk hand in hand with spiritual salvation.

Peter Singer in his book The Life You Can Save speaks of an image of a person drowning in a pool of water. We stand there, knowing that we can help, but we don't want to get our hair or new clothes wet. So we decide to stretch out our hand and shout for the person to grab hold of it, but we find that they are too far away. The moral of the story is simply this: we are trying to help but our effort falls short of what is really needed. We need to jump into the water and get what we cherish "wet".

The demonstration of the Gospel requires more than our outstretched hand while remaining within our comfortable surroundings. Sometimes lifestyle choices, work routines, spending habits and time schedules need to be uprooted and put upon the balancing scales of how much we are affected by the pain around us. Our compassion does not necessarily demand dramatic history-changing events. Sometimes all that is needed is a simple act of love or encouragement.

Before the emergence and now global praise for the Salvation Army's work, William struggled with being rejected by those around him. "Even a tentative application to sign on as Chaplain in a convict hulk bound for Botany Bay, a ministry from which most clerics fought shy, had been turned down." With his latest rejection of a renewal ticket for him to preach in Walworths Methodist Chapel, this young preacher had nowhere to turn, and was tempted to divert his attention back upon his work profession of a pawn-broker. But a businessman named Edward Harris Rabbits invited him back to his home for dinner. Taking time to encourage William about the fire of God that he was so visually carrying, he spurred him on to devote everything to the preaching of the Gospel. And for the first few months he agreed that he would cover William's living expenses.

Spurred on, William then moved into two cramped rooms in a widows' house in London. And with Rabbits' encouragement again, he attended a Reformers' meeting on his twenty-third birthday, that led to the introduction to his future wife and work partner, Catherine.

This small narrative leaves us with a beautiful encouragement. To jump into the pool and "get wet" with what God is stirring within us does not always make for big, dramatic, close-up moments. Instead we find it sewn into the very fabric of people's lives, where one person's journey is also made up of a mosaic of gentle miraculous interactions that all play a part. Our inner motivation is worshipfully stirred by His compassion, as we serve in ways that surprise even ourselves.

Moments to reflect

"I always thank my God as I remember you in my prayers,
because I hear about your faith in the Lord Jesus and the love for all the saints.
I pray that you may be active in sharing your faith,
so that you will have a full understanding of every good thing we have in Christ.
Your love has given me great joy and encouragement,
because you, brother, have refreshed the hearts of the saints."

(Philemon 1:4-7 NIV)

"To make our weak hearts strong and brave,
send the fire.
To live a dying world to save,
send the fire today.
Oh see us on Your altar lay,
we give our lives to You today.
So crown the offering now we pray,
send the fire today."

Send The Fire by William Booth, 1894

Prayer:

"Help me, dear Lord, to know that my act of love to this needy world is a precious offering in worship – an offering that is not to be compared to those around, but lived out in peaceful assurance. Thank you that these acts of love are an integral part of Your story of Love. Let no jealousy or pride come my way, but may simple joy and thanksgiving consume my life, as I join in with my fellow family, praising You in all the threads of my being."

21: Behind The Curtain

"Pay no attention to that man behind the curtain.
The Great Oz has spoken!"

The Wizard Of Oz, 1939 musical film

From the pen of L. Frank Baum's original 1900 novel to Victor Fleming's famous film adaptation in 1939, the story of "The Wonderful Wizard Of Oz" has captured the hearts and imaginations of both young and old. Colourful and dynamic images of adventure fill its retelling, taking the listener on a journey of hope and friendship as they follow the mismatched group of travellers en route to see the renowned wizard of Oz. As they finally get an audience in the Emerald City, they are confronted with a mighty display of the powerful wizard. But in such a marvellous description of how small actions can have dramatic implications, Dorothy's dog knocks over the screen (or pulls at the curtain, depending on whether it's the book or the film) revealing an elderly man who is pulling all the levers to create a show of strength and power.

This childhood story creates a wonderful image: that there is something behind the display of lights and powerful demonstrations we see in front of us. There is a curtain that hides hidden levers that make the visual spectacle happen. A simple reminder that while the outward looks exciting and appealing, the strength and force of what we see in front lies somewhere else.

Charles McCallon Alexander was born in Tennessee in 1867. Married to Helen Cadbury (the daughter of Richard Cadbury, president of Cadbury Chocolate Company) Alexander became famous as an evangelist and gospel singer who toured with

R.A. Torrey, another American writer and preacher. After taking inspiration from Helen's work of encouraging girls to sew pockets onto their dresses so they could carry a copy of the New Testament, pledging to read a portion each day, he launched the Pocket Testament League into a wider setting. Reaching countless people in many countries, his passion for the Gospel bypassed the confinements of war, social boundaries and political settings.

As the title of his wife's book highlights; *Charles M. Alexander: A romance of song and soul-winning*, his story and his efforts had far-reaching effects. The fragrance of his walk continues to linger through to current history. Yet behind this wondrous display lies another story, just as beautiful and intimately entwined into the famous outworking of his life.

Charles' father, a singer and violinist, taught him to read music and appreciate the diversity in tones and rhythm. His mother read sermons to him by the American Evangelist D. L. Moody, and took time to teach him scripture. It is said that he first read the entire Bible through by the age of nine. The death of his father prompted deep soul searching and, finding new assurance in the promise of heaven, Alexander then went to the Moody Bible Institute. After his training he served with such individuals as Billy Sunday and Dr. Reuben Archer Torrey. Learning from them and supporting their works with his knowledge and qualification of music, he was a real asset to their missions together. A trip to the UK allowed him to meet his future wife, Helen, a partnership that would support their respective journeys and their walk together.

The life of Charles Alexander is the story that we all share in some way. All of us have occasions and exchanges that speak of something deeply precious, yet often unseen and unnoticed at the time. God invests in the intricate beauty of the "levers" behind the curtain of our lives, ensuring that it is His power we tap into, not our own. He weaves our interconnecting stories carefully to bless us, and those around us, for our good and His glory.

But it is the simple, mundane routines that hold such importance. Lines in texts and emails, conversations over washing up, pats on the shoulder in the street – these are the gentle, unsung marks of the miraculous; moments that show how we choose to spend our money, work out our resources and decide our rightful work patterns. Each of these seemingly insignificant days hang with great relevance as each scene starts to hint at the space we inhabit for His praise.

Our lives, in all their littleness, are a beautiful masterpiece of heavenly work, that Charles Alexander sang so powerfully about in The Glory Song. Reminding us that our steps today carry the brushstrokes of His love, our daily interactions strengthen ourselves and others with armour for the onward journey. Pulling back the curtain within our heart we can see the levers of His love, the force that motivates our actions, sacrifices and commitments to one another.

Moments to reflect

"If you have any encouragement from being united with Christ,
if any comfort from His love, if any fellowship with the Spirit,
If any tenderness and compassion,
then make my joy complete by being like-minded,
having the same love, being one in spirit and purpose.
Do nothing out of selfish ambition or vain conceit,
but in humility consider others better than yourselves.
Each of you should look not only to your own interests, but also to
the interests of others.
Your attitude should be the same as that of Christ Jesus."

(Philippians 2:1-5 NIV)

"Friends will be there I have loved long ago;
Joy like a river around me will flow.
Yet, just a smile from my Saviour, I know.
Will thro' the ages be glory for me.
O that will be glory for me.
Glory for me, glory for me.
When by His grace I shall look on His face.
That will be glory, be glory for me."

O That Will Be Glory (also known as The Glory Song),
Charles H. Gabriel, 1900

Prayer:

"Precious Lord, the masterful painter of life, thank you for the tiny, colourful parts of the canvas of my life. May I appreciate each moment I live, seeing beauty and treasure in the small things. Remind me that my steps speak of higher things than those valued by the world. Whether acclaimed or hidden from sight, I find comforting peace in this hope. Help me to continue to walk in a way that echoes Your attitude and speaks of Your heart. Teach me to rest in the assurance that my worth is truly found in You."

22: The Hidden Landscape

"Travel is fatal to prejudice, bigotry and narrow-mindedness,
and many of our people need it sorely on these accounts.
Broad, wholesome, charitable views of men and things,
cannot be acquired by vegetating in one little corner
of the earth all one's lifetime."

Mark Twain, The Innocents Abroad

When we stand on a mountain top we see God's generous and lavish creative powers before us. The inspiration that suddenly floods our souls is palpable and precious. As we travel we stare out of train or plane windows to watch an unfolding story of beauty, colour, life and purpose – every cloud, every flower, every leaf designed. Moments like these speak of something bigger, deeper, wider, declaring in all their tones and shades that our perception touches just a part of a wider terrain.

Our senses are wonderful tools for exploration and yet they are limited. A wonderful analogy was once told to me that seems to perfectly speak of things that are hidden from one's initial gaze. Imagine standing by a lake and observing its still waters. As our eyes glance over this liquid landscape we see little bits of land protruding through like miniature icebergs. If, for a special moment, we could drain its water like pulling a plug out from its deep floor, we would see a different image emerge before our eyes – a landscape that has always been there, but until the water was lowered, remained hidden from our sight.

These two differing terrains co-exist, but one is hidden from view. Each carries its own identity, but is also wrapped into the other's display. For us this image brings with it a moment of reflection upon our own journey and what we choose to value.

In a town near Manchester, England, 2009, a small group of people came together in a room – just under a dozen in total. This was not a church building, but a renovated workshop and stock room. The meeting room was situated on the top floor – a small office with an odd collection of chairs that had been gathered from donations and purchases.

As they all sat around in a circle, one could not escape the diverse collection of backgrounds they all represented – a "chalk-and-cheese" gathering of viewpoints and lives – from a professional businessperson wearing a suit that cost more than some had made in the last two months to an individual who was living in a squat. They met to bear witness to a growing tribe that was gathering there, from the young social radical who had worked on a number of ground level protests concerning injustice to the shy person who found their way of helping people was through cooking meals and giving them away one-by-one.

Each person told their story, expressing their dreams and beliefs, opening up about the struggles and then balancing it out with the joys of seeing God come through. No matter the wealth of the person, the size of their project, or whether it made the front pages of any news report, they all had one thing in common: they had all chosen to express God's love on the path of normality that His hand had led them on.

At the end of the sharing, a holy moment descended. An awareness of what the group had heard was expressed. Found within this little room of odd chairs and diverse individuals was an image of overlapping stories and mutual relationships that, until then, had not be seen, heard or tasted. Here was a landscape of distinctive actions, yet they all blended together into a multi-dimensional expression of one story: the story of God.

How wonderful to have that water drained away and to experience the landscape from a new perspective! We are all set in our field of vision at times: the groupings of people we relate with, the reading material that mirrors our preferences in theology, the good works that our local congregation is doing . . . our horizons can be mirages of boundaries not actually there.

And in only the way our creative Lord can do, He adjusts our perception as we stop and stare at the landscape before us, observing what we have grown accustomed to, then helping us to look again to what we didn't see before. Now our eyes are widened, our understanding is heightened: differing terrains, but also one. He leads us to rejoice in His craftsmanship, knowing that our own visions, dreams and hopes carry a DNA that interlinks each of us, one with the other – the multi-dimensional unity that is His miraculous body.

Moments to reflect

"And let us consider
how we may spur one another on toward love and good deeds.
Let us not give up meeting together,
as some are in the habit of doing,
but let us encourage one another . . ."
(Hebrews 10:24-25 NIV)

"Open the eyes of my heart Lord.
Open the eyes of my heart.
I want to see You. I want to see You."

Open The Eyes Of My Heart by Paul Baloche
Integrity Music Inc © 2000

Prayer:

"Precious Lord, open my eyes to the wondrous vista laid before me – a landscape that holds such dimensions, shades and tones of Your love in action. Enable me to start seeing the interlinking paths of each pilgrim of the cross, to value their contribution and the worth that they carry. Give me the wisdom not to pre-judge others or live in a self-important world. Help me to find worth in each story not just my own."

23: Servants of the Cross
and Not of Our Labours

"It was thought by persons here that the state of things in our
church demanded my presence. Had it not been for this
pressure, we should have remained longer in England.
I thought then, and think now, that the work would have
greatly increased, not only in Manchester, but throughout all
that part of England, could we have remained another year
or two. But as I said, we were over-ruled by the intelligence
from this place, and left England with great reluctance,
hoping that sometime we might return."

The Memoirs of Charles G. Finney
(Ch36, Return to Oberlin and Glorious Revival)

The life of Charles Grandison Finney carries great admiration
in many circles. His strong character and determination to
passionately see that the Gospel message was experienced in real
and tangible ways, continues to stir hearts two hundred years
later. The blessings that flowed from his work with community
partnerships and social concern groups still inspire similar stories.
His memoirs radiate with the beauty of how the Spirit of God
flowed through the work of his hands.

Found within his writings is an account concerning his focus
upon England. Finney visited England believing revival was
possible and timely. After 12 months of mission he set sail back
to America in 1860. As he boarded the ship he seemed remorseful
in leaving, feeling that if he had stayed for another year or two
then more things could have happened and developed.

It leads us to ask, why did he leave? Why set sail back home when he felt his personal involvement had yet to be finished? The answer I am sure has many strands, some hidden and some plain to see, and it would be an injustice to try to paint a whole picture on assumptions and opinions. So we are left with colours of the moment; hints made and statements written that bring some sort of shape to what we see. One such colour he alluded to gave a challenge not only to readers and hearers of that time, but to each one of us in this moment of today – that of the "construct" that called him back.

Our journey within this life brings many opportunities to establish structures that support our passions and dreams. Done out of a pure motive to gird up what God has placed within us, we plan out lines of operation and good practice. There is nothing wrong with these, and we can find them deeply helpful within our walk. Yet the fiery and deeply compassionate pilgrim of our faith told a story of his life that makes us all consider what we erect.

He was welcoming the later months of his time here on earth, and had taken those moments to share his story. He had lived through various community awakenings within the British Isles, and found it a joy to recount those blessed moments. Asked why he felt one of those awakenings that he was sharing about had ended, tears welled up inside his eyelids. His response was not like many of his stories that were long, deviating down many "rabbit holes" of thoughts and memories. Instead, it was short and to the point. His response was that he didn't really know in full, but one thing he observed was that before the awakening, the prayer meetings had more people in them than the celebration gatherings. When it ended, those celebration gatherings had more people in them than the prayer meetings. He then ended his answer with this thought: "that the very thing that first connected our hearts to our Lord got superseded by the fruits of our labours."

The problem does not lie in the structures themselves. The celebration gatherings were an integral part of the sharing of the Gospel message. Neither was Finney, or his Bible school back in Oberlin which urged him to leave England, suggesting that he did anything wrong. His return home stirred a great response and the work from that college laid foundational stones for students to work in the fields of mission all over the world. Instead, this aging storyteller moved from pointing fingers and replaced it with the challenge of the balancing act that is constant within all our lives: that the thing we construct to serve our journey and vision can so easily itself become the very thing we serve.

It's a delicate tiptoeing journey to ensure that the frameworks we construct amplify the Message we proclaim, but do not impinge on it. Our goal must be to hold firmly to a vision, while also being in a continual state of willingness to lay all that scaffolds it at His feet. Being servants of His cross and not of our works seems such a simple statement to verbalise, yet it is a constant battle to make sure our hearts always sing this song: that humble and worshipful surrender is more miraculous in heaven's eyes than all the successes of man.

Moments to reflect

"Pursue righteousness, godliness, faith, love, patience, gentleness.
Fight the good fight of faith, lay hold on eternal life,
to which you were also called and have confessed the good confession
in the presence of many witnesses.
I urge you in the sight of God who gives life to all things,
and before Christ Jesus who witnessed the good confession before
Pontius Pilate,
that you keep this commandment without spot,

blameless until our Lord Jesus Christ's appearing,
which He will manifest in His own time,
He who is the blessed and only Potentate, the King of kings and
Lord of lords,
who alone has immortality, dwelling in unapproachable light,
whom no man has seen or can see,
to who be honour and everlasting power. Amen."

(1 Timothy 6:11-16 NKJV)

"Every day I see more of Your greatness.
Every day I know more of my weakness . . .
For the eyes of my heart,
they're on You for ever, they're on You forever."

Eyes Of My Heart by Tim Hughes
Worship Together © 2001

Prayer:

"Father, I ask for Your guiding Hand upon my life. Helping me maintain the balance of my commitment to Your calling, while keeping my eyes firmly set upon You. Being driven with determination to finish the race, but finding my energy being drawn from my embrace of Your cross, help me to carry all the hallmarks of a true friend of Yours. May my witness not be by any empty works, but in the fullness of Your life flowing through me.

24: Bigger And More Exciting

"Airport '77,
the tradition of motion picture excitement continues.
Bigger, more exciting than Airport '75."

Movie Trailer for Airport '77

When I first heard the trailer tagline to this movie it made me smile. It seemed to sum up the 70s disaster movie scene in a perfect sound-bite – as something exciting, big and monumental that must not be missed. And more importantly, as something more thrilling and riveting than the film screened two years previously. On one hand it was just a classic film introduction that was there to capture one's attention, but the underlying tone behind those words reveals something far deeper for us.

Wrapped up in the journey of the 19th century preacher William "Billy" Bray are stories of individuals who contributed to his pursuit of seeing salvation in the land. One of them was a character simply known as "Grandfather". He had asked Billy if he could come with him to a teetotal meeting that he was holding just outside Newlyn, Cornwall. The only problem was that he was almost a cripple, struggling with great pain as he walked. So Billy stopped and prayed for him and a wonderful miracle took place. As they arrived at the meeting, Grandfather sang out a hymn and gave testimony to how he used to be a drunk, but was now a teetotaller, saved and happy. Billy then followed and at the conclusion, 20 people signed the Pledge. The following week after Billy had spoken at another meeting in Newlyn, Grandfather stood up again and gave testimony to how he once was lame and suffering with pain, but now was living a life of healing and comfort.

It is a wonderful thing to read those accounts that are wrapped up inside the famous and more recognisable moments in history, where our gaze is changed to look at something in the background. There is real worth in the conversations and individual journeys, a value that could be so easily lost amidst our pursuit for the seminal moments.

Those life-changing days are, of course, very powerful, having an excitement and impact that is like throwing a big stone into a pond. The noise of its splash echoes down the years, providing ripples of remembrance that give us encouragement, energising our walk. But sometimes it is the small pebbles thrown into water that have the longest and furthest-reaching ripples.

In times of reflection as we breathe in those big or little moments, our senses come alive with another fragrance as well. Its bouquet is subtle, but unavoidable, helping us see that our story is the priceless image of God at work. Each of us declare by the way we live our lives that it doesn't matter whether we are making a big splash in the pond of history or telling a simple God-story around a dining room table – all of our lives speak of the same thing. Our journeys tell of the relentlessly diverse and creatively colourful nature and purpose of God soaking into this land.

If we can truly grasp this truth, it changes the very depiction we see as we look at ourselves in our mind's mirror. The reflected likeness that plays back our actions, abilities and thoughts, both internal and verbally declared, does not need to be graded or compared to others around. We don't need to polish the mirror glass or find a higher watt bulb to change what we see. Instead we just see ourselves in full form in all our flaws and fabulousness. It shines beyond all of that, over and above the mismatch of all our thoughts and hopes deferred; strengths that can be praised and admired, and those elements of our life that hold a secret shame that we long to change. In this very centre we are wonderfully, miraculously loved and totally accepted.

Sometimes it is easy for us to think that God is looking for the next big thing or the next important person. But we don't need to impress God with some exciting ability or great initiative. We just need to be ourselves with all our silly moments and profound statements. His gaze is already firmly set upon us, transfixed and unwavering.

And as we rest upon this beautiful truth of our worth, our spirits can rejoice in the revealing of Himself within all of the layers and interactions of our lives. Each step we make is vital and intrinsic to His story. But there is no name in lights for us. No central billing or top stars are required, except that of Christ who takes centre stage.

And what is the tagline for this great love story? The very life you and I are living right now. The miracle of the normal Christian life.

Moments to reflect

"Show the wonder of Your great love,
You who save by Your right hand those who take refuge in You
from their foes.
Keep me as the apple of Your eye;
hide me in the shadow of Your wings."

(Psalm 17:7-8 NIV)

"This is yet another prayer song.
Sometimes I find it hard to pray, maybe that's why I written so many prayer songs.
'Cause it is easier to sing sometimes,
God may find them more entertaining than if you just say it to –
who knows.

Except I am not really all that sure that God is concerned about
being entertained,
if that's just a human thing.
Sometimes you try to pray, try to impress God with all
the right words.
I just don't think it's an easy thing to impress God Almighty.
And here is the thing I think we often forget – we don't have to
impress Him.
He is already knocked out about you, already loves you more
than you can imagine."

Rich Mullins, talk intro for the song
Step by Step from Here In America DVD

Prayer:

"What more could I ask for, than this wonderful truth that I
am loved? The apple of Your eye, the centre of Your attention,
covered by the shadow of Your wings. A love that is not earned,
or in need of being impressed – it is a love that is indescribable –
that surpasses my greatest imagination. Teach my life to kiss the
things that You kiss, O Lord, to pay attention to what You pay
attention to. Let my heart gradually take in each precious
action and attitude of Your love so that I may not miss a single
dewdrop of Your Presence. May each act of service made in Your
name mirror your love for the lost, last and least in this world in
which I have been placed."

25: Stature Of Love's Embrace

"I realised that God had done something for that man that He hadn't done for me. When he started preaching I was sorry for him, but when he got through I was sorry for myself."

Branham's account recorded in William Branham:
A Man Sent By God by Gordon Lindsay

There is a wonderful account of an aging preacher whose sermon influenced a young listener. This youthful person only saw him once, and his name was never remembered. Yet what shone through that preacher's life remained with this man for a lifetime and became a pivotal point in the early years of God's calling upon his destiny.

This young man was called William M. Branham, who in later years would be heavily associated with the faith healing movement of the 1930's and beyond. Both during his life, and after his death in 1965, his ministry divided opinion. Yet regardless of where a commentator stands, one can't avoid a beautiful description that Branham recounted, recorded by Gordon Lindsay, as he retold the moment he saw that aging preacher.

"The following afternoon they had an old man get up and preach. He was rather decrepit and I was a little surprised to see them choose such a fellow to preach before that great congregation. He preached from the text, 'Where were you when I laid the foundations of the earth, when the morning stars sang together'. Well, that old fellow picked up about ten million years before the world was ever formed. He just about covered everything in heaven, came down the horizontal rainbow and preached on everything on earth up till the Second Coming of Christ. By the time he had finished he was as spry as a young man. In fact he said, as he went down from the platform, 'You haven't got room enough for me to preach.' I realised that God had done something for that man that He hadn't done for me. When he started preaching I was sorry for him, but when he got through I was sorry for myself."

There is something that words seem to fall short of describing when it comes to the wealth of faith that each one of us holds – a grace in our lives that marinates and soaks through all that we are, where no matter what show or front we put up, the mirror of our life starts to reflect the depth of what lies within.

A few years back a story was recounted of an evangelistic meeting that was held for a local community and neighbourhood. A special speaker and travelling party was called in to give the keynote talk, supplying the final element to a month-long-mission. It had created quite a buzz and had drawn great interest. So as the chairs started to be filled, the sound in the old hall became dense with the collation of mumblings, comments and hushed conversations.

The start of the gathering went as planned. Stories were told, music performed and presentations were made of the good works that had happened over weeks past. But as the minutes continued, no visible response was apparent from the listening crowd. Some of the members of the congregations who had put this mission on started to think it was all over. Even their keynote speaker, who had brought many laughs and gasps in previous meetings, could not break the sense of a spiritual stone wall around those present.

Then a young teenage girl made her way to the front. Some recognised her and had seen her around before, while others questioned themselves as to whether she was a part of their own local congregation or had visited their neighbourhood shops. Nobody quite knew what to do, as this was not part of the order of service. But by stopping a girl as she took the stage, you could end up looking like the villain, so everyone just watched as she stood in front of the waiting crowd, then simply sang the song, Jesus loves me this I know.

A hushed silence transformed into the sound of tears, as men and women of all ages began to cry. Not everyone in the room cried, but enough did for all to recognise that something special was happening. People were transfixed on the passion radiating from her, a young teenage girl who genuinely believed she was loved by her Saviour. And when she had finished, there was no need for an altar call or indeed any words to be spoken. People simply responded there and then to the calling of the Lord.

The man who told me that story, recounted it in such a way that it seemed only yesterday to him. But in fact, it happened over forty years earlier when he was just starting out as a preacher. The beauty of what he saw that night taught him a lesson that remained alive within him for the following decades. It became a parable that he taught to anyone who dared to listen, a simple truth that no one could deny.

The parable was this: if we truly believe, people WILL see Him! If the passion of Christ runs through our being, people WILL see Him! If we count all the world's gains as loss and embrace the prosperity of heaven's embrace, people WILL see Him! That girl, singing her heart out, allowed others to respond with their own hearts. God needed nothing more to break through.

Moments to reflect

"Therefore, I urge you, brothers,
in view of God's mercy, to offer your bodies as living sacrifices,
holy and pleasing to God – this is your spiritual act of worship.
Do not conform any longer to the pattern of this world,

but be transformed by the renewing of your mind.
Then you will be able to test and approve what God's will is,
His good, pleasing and perfect will."

(Romans 12:1-2 NIV)

"I wanna shine the light You gave, thru Your Son You sent
to save us.
From ourselves and our despair, it comforts me to know You're
really there.
I wanna die and let You give, Your life to me so I might live.
And share the hope You gave to me, the love that set me free.
I wanna tell the world out there, You're not some fable or fairy tale.
That I've made up inside my head.
You're God the Son and You've risen from the dead."

Make My Life A Prayer To You by Keith Green
Sparrow © 1999

Prayer:

"I yearn for my life to be a prayer to You, O Lord – each action,
thought and deed moulded from a worshipful heart. As your
light gets stronger and You increase, so my status dims and what
matters changes. Help me to sing loudly in my life of Your great
love in ways that break strongholds and take captive hearts that
long for more. I acknowledge that in both the big and the small,
my endeavours and plans lay ruined without Your Hand."

26: How We See Victory

"Defeat may serve as well as victory
To shake the soul and let the glory out.
When the great oak is straining in the wind
The limbs drink in new beauty, and the trunk sends
down a deeper root on the windward side."

L.B. Cowman, Streams In The Desert (January 18th entry)

A man who had faithfully served his Christian community, country and the mission fields abroad, took time out to consider his filled years of life. Deeply aware of the second hand of time that was starting to slow down, he wanted to impart what he had learnt, discovered and observed to those of another generation. The awaiting listeners were aware of some of the exciting stories that he had been a part of, heightening expectations for insights and behind-the-scenes conversations, as well as the potential of new tales of godly adventure.

Instead, they were greeted with an unusual statement: "Sometimes things are not always what they seem." He followed that up with a series of narratives where he had followed the promptings of the Lord, only to find that the visual results of his actions embodied more defeat and failure than victory. They were stories, accounts and examples of how God's ways were higher, deeper and wider than his own set of rules and expectations for success.

As he recounted his tales he spoke of how some things – a prophetic word given or project set up – had all the trappings of fulfilment and obvious blessing. Yet this was also married with accounts of how he had struggled behind the scenes, away from the crowd's gaze and in secret ways that didn't help his public persona.

In the solemn silence of this small group, he ended with words that pointed towards the cross – the cross that speaks of beauty in ugliness, or forgiveness in the midst of sin, of healing in hurting and of struggle in sacrifice. The cross speaks of ways higher than ours, thoughts higher than ours and understanding no one can fathom. It messes with the way we think things should go.

Etched within history and faith is an account of a man who approached a tree that would lead to the apparent end of his life. Over such short years he had spoken of the freedom that captivated the hearts of those around and disturbed the forces that had ruled over the downtrodden. Large crowds followed and rumblings within the corridors of power fuelled expectations of what would happen next. He was a healer, prophet, poet, wordsmith – someone who demonstrated compassion in such exquisite ways that gave hope to many around. His reference to liberty and signs of heavenly power started people talking about whether he was the One spoken about of old: their Saviour and Redeemer, who would finally deliver them from all oppression.

The gathered support for this message of hope had grown. Surely this increased group of followers held the potential of being galvanised into a powerful fighting force? Yet none of it seemed to matter now. The hope of victory had faded, as this on-looking crowd saw their supposed Saviour hanging dead upon a cross that was erected by the very people He was supposed to save them from.

We know the continuation of this story – the glorious victory and full salvation that our resurrected Lord bought for us. Yet imagine those days before the miracle of the rolled away stone, where the chosen path of victory was one that defied expectation and logical sense. Would we have run away in disbelief or buried ourselves deep in disillusionment? Maybe we would have reacted in the opposite way, taking our anger out on the nearby guards or trying to rouse the awaiting crowd into a fighting army?

The man telling his story knew moments of confusion and had lived through many emotional attempts of trying to make sense of the path of the cross for himself. Yet in it all, he had found tranquillity in the assurance that being a follower of Christ is not always about knowing why. The journey may not always make sense, but it is continually bathed in the light of faith, found in love. For him, that was enough. Is it enough for you?

There is an invitation to us all to cherish both the moments we understand and those that rest upon nothing more than deep trust in the darkness – being at peace that sometimes His leading will challenge our own expectations, causing unrest within our flesh but nourishment to our soul; where our sight could be upon freedom from a group of soldiers, while His could be upon the liberation of all creation.

Moments to reflect

"I don't think the way you think.
The way you work isn't the way I work.
God's decree.
For as the sky soars high above earth,
so the way I work surpasses the way you work,
and the way I think is beyond the way you think.
Just as rain and snow descend from the skies
and don't go back until they've watered the earth,
doing their work of making things grow and blossom,
producing seed for farmers and food for the hungry.
So will the words that come out of My mouth not come back
empty-handed.

they'll do the work I sent them to do, they'll complete the assignment
I gave them.
So you'll go out in joy, you'll be led into a whole and complete life."

(Isaiah 55:8-12 The Message)

"I lay myself at Your feet.
Asking You, won't You meet.
I cannot do it on my own.
I cannot do it all alone."

Here I Am by Shawn McDonald
Sparrow © 2004

Prayer:

"I will not pretend Lord. Sometimes the inner battle of my mind rages against the leading of Your Spirit. My personal expectations strive to find dominance. I jostle for position with You don't I? So I admit defeat and say again that You are all I need, all I ever desired and all I choose. Help me find the joy of the surrendered life and to live it in a way that impacts all within my circle. Teach me that your ways are not just higher than mine, but better than mine."

27: Partnership of Our Dreams

"The revival in South Wales is not of men, but of God.
He has come very close to us.

... I am not the source of the revival, but only an agent
among what is a growing multitude.

... Many who are now silent Christians will lead the
movement. They will see a great light and will reflect
this light to thousands now in darkness."

Letter from Evan Roberts, 1905 (Azusa Street, Frank Bartleman)

Caught up in the chronicles of the Azusa Street Revival history
is a brief account of Joseph Smale – the pastor of a local Baptist
church in Los Angeles, who, being stirred by the reports of the
Welsh Revival, went to visit the country of Wales to experience
first-hand what was happening. Upon his return he was stirred
to, "have the same visitations and blessings come to his own
church." So, joining in with a chorus of prayer meetings that
were already happening around the city, his own meetings
ran for fifteen weeks until he was asked by the church officials
to either stop this pursuit or resign. September 1905 saw his
resignation, but he continued his pursuit in prayer and the eventual
establishment of another congregation. Seven months later, history
focuses our attention upon the famous April 1906 events with
William J. Seymour.

Brother Smale, like many others, embraced a journey of both
joy and sacrifice for what was stirring in his heart. The outworking
of his hope may not have happened in the way he had originally
envisioned, and an onlooker's gaze may focus on others who
followed afterwards. Yet his story is intrinsic not only to the early

years of the twentieth century, but to where we all stand today, reminding us of the partnership of our individual dreams, so beautifully described by the words of Frank Bartleman: "God found His Moses in the person of Brother Smale to lead us to the Jordan crossing. But He chose Brother Seymour, for our Joshua to lead us over."

What a breathtaking life we embrace – that we are dreamers, people of hope and pilgrims of faith who have been given such a wondrous gift: to become lost in a series of hopes and ideas, no matter the size or perception. And while some of these dreams may "yet to be", they can still be seen as our goal in the mind's eye. Moulding our life's direction around them with passionate commitment, we are spurred on towards the hope laid out before us.

And in our passion to serve our loving God, we may take what He is stirring and interpret its outworking in many ways: a show of strength, a commitment towards a cause, maybe a written down vision or road map of a goal. None are wrong and our motives may come from a worshiping heart, but these cherished dreams connect us to something far deeper than our best-laid plans.

The clear waters of God's purposes for us invite us not only to dip in, but to immerse ourselves into their flow and currents, encouraging us to look past the sound of our own voice and lean our ear towards a heavenly heartbeat. And as we spend time in worship, the very essence of God's presence soaks into our dreams. It speaks of the precious and vulnerable element that our dreams and passions carry: that our hopes are not fulfilled in our own strength.

It is truly a marvellous moment of our faith when our ear tunes itself to the sound of a wider unity alongside of our Christian family – a heavenly composition that can only be conducted by the hand of God. Some may find their own works praised within history, others may see their life's service towards a dream fulfilled in someone else. But whatever the outcome, there is only One true destination that we are all heading towards.

His name is Jesus.

Moments to reflect

"I praise you because I am fearfully and wonderfully made;
your works are wonderful, I know that full well.
My frame was not hidden from you when I was made in the secret place.
When I was woven together in the depths of the earth,
your eyes saw my unformed body.
All the days ordained for me were written in your book
before one of them came to be.
How precious to me are your thoughts, O God!
How vast is the sum of them!"

(Psalm 139:14-17 NIV)

"Alone we can do so little;
together we can do so much."

To Love This Life by Helen Keller
(Scholastic Paperbacks, 2002)

Prayer:

"Thank you, loving God for the truth that I am fearfully and wonderfully made, that the life I live is part of an unfolding story of Your creativity. Thank you for the gifts, abilities and treasures you have placed in me. Teach me to use them, develop them and hone them in your service. In my excitement of knowing

Your fingerprints upon my life, may I never lose sight of the hope of Your beauty and purpose being fully revealed alongside my brothers and sisters. Help me to partner with You and them in a way that pleases Your heart."

28: Just One Touch From The King

"Love Divine, all loves excelling.
Joy of heaven, to earth come down.
Fix in us Thy humbly dwelling.
All Thy faithful mercies crown."

Love Divine All Loves Excelling, lyrics by Charles Wesley

John Graham Lake is a recognised character in many circles of our faith. Born in 1870, saved through The Salvation Army, influenced by the ministry of John Alexander Dowie (a healing evangelist and founder of the American city Zion, Illinois), and affected by the happenings within the Azusa Street Revival, he set his sights upon being a missionary to South Africa in 1908. During the next five years, over 700 churches were planted with many accounts of miracles taking place. Moving back to America in 1913, he established the Healing Rooms in Spokane, Washington in 1914 and Portland, Oregon in 1920, as well as many healing campaigns until his departure from this life in 1935.

Hundreds of thousands of miracles were recorded during that time, and people of all backgrounds got involved in spreading the wider message of God's healing touch. One such moment is recorded in Lake's April 22nd, 1917 sermon. It recounts the story of Mrs Annie E. Norton who, while cutting a ham with a saw, cut through her first forefinger to the bone. This led over the next few days to her arm becoming paralysed, which some first thought was gangrene. Dr O'Neil who was in charge of the case soon discovered it was something else that he did not know.

The disease was spreading, even with the amputation of her arm. No remedies were found, so they eased her pain through narcotics, until she eventually became dependent on morphine. The following years saw great strain upon the family both in physical and financial terms. By the time she had lost her sight, over seven hundred physicians had examined her, still with no solution to her infirmity.

Sown into this setting is the story of two women: one a widow and the other married, both with five children apiece. They visited Mrs Norton on a number of occasions, kneeling by the side of her bed, "not anxious about the subject of her healing", but "anxious that this soul should not pass into the other life without the consciousness and support of Jesus Christ, a present Saviour."

Mrs Norton gave her heart to Christ as she heard her name being spoken by the Lord. She instantly felt her pain go away, with signs of mortification and rottenness of flesh eradicated, as life was brought back into her body. That moment was the 23rd September, 1916, the date when she became a well woman once again. Her case was discussed by many groups of people, including the British Medical Journal. Mrs Norton herself would travel around recounting the wonderful testimony of her healing. Found within the fabric of this story, behind its scenes, are two prayerful women with ten children between them.

In amongst glorious accounts of God moving, we can find countless examples of the normal interactions made by followers of Christ, where a thoughtful act of compassion becomes another channel of God's miracle-working power. A show of mercy, a demonstration of love, a proactive desire to hold onto the best for someone close – nothing is ignored by His loving hand.

A powerful peace can surround our hearts as we acknowledge that there is nothing too small to be useful in His kingdom. There is a deep and profound beauty in the knowledge that just one touch from the King changes everything – a touch that originates from His love and care for each one of us.

Love surpasses all descriptive words, its motivating force leading to the most dramatic of sacrifices and humblest of actions. It gently leads us as we learn to become those who live a life of "EXTRA-ordinariness". The call on our lives is for us to be men and women who see past the filtered lens of earthly comparisons and begin to find clarity through His heart towards each other. My prayer for you is that wherever you touch the world, you would do so not just with your fingers, but with His.

Moments to reflect

"Then the King will say to those on His right.
Come, you who are blessed by my Father;
take your inheritance, the kingdom prepared for you since the creation of this world.
For I was hungry and you gave me something to eat,
I was thirsty and you gave me something to drink,
I was a stranger and you invited me in,
I needed clothes and you clothed me,
I was sick and you looked after me,
I was in prison and you came to visit me.
. . . I tell you the truth,
whatever you did for one of the least of these brothers of mine, you did for Me."

(Matthew 25:34-36-40 NIV)

"Now this roof has got a few missing shingles. But at least we got ourselves a roof.
And they say that she's a fallen angel. I wonder if she recalls when she last flew.
There's no point in pointing fingers. Unless you're pointing to the truth.

And I will be my brother's keeper. Not the one who judges him.
I won't despise him for his weakness. I won't regard him
for his strength.
I won't take away his freedom. I will help him learn to stand.
And I will, I will be my brother's keeper."

Brother's Keeper by Rich Mullins
BMG Music © 1995

Prayer:

"Loving God and merciful Saviour, no dictionary is able to define You, no book can describe You. You pursue us with all Your being, making a way for us to find hope once again. In all that I do let my prayer be this: that I would work as Your servant to those around me as my brother's keeper and defender, not his judge or critic. Forgive me for the many times I have wasted my life in expectations born out of selfish desires and teach me to honour Your ways above my own."

29: Above All Else

"From His goodness, His loving-kindness
His good-natured benevolence, God does it!
That's the source of everything."

A. W. Tozer, The Attributes of God

I cannot think of a better way to end this work than to rest upon a moment that greatly influenced this whole collection of words. During a visit to the Isle of Lewis, where I had arranged to spend time with some individuals who had lived through a past move of God, I came across a small, broken china ornament that had Psalm 23 painted on it.

I found it during one of the trips around this cold, windy island that a wonderful man of God took me on. We ended up at a broken-down house that is rarely mentioned in the history books, but beautifully symbolises the reality of those who sacrificially served God to see their community changed. The family who had lived there used their home as a space for prayer and retreat, and a space to mobilise active service to people in need.

Pushing my way through a gap in the fence, I entered into this crumbling ruin. It was damp and filled with the stale smell of rotting furniture. Scattered around were remnants of the family. A few water-soaked pictures were still hanging up on the wall, a worn armchair – the kind that reminded me of those a father would sit in as he read the evening paper. The kitchen had a few odd pans and plates and an old baking bowl that would have been used for the morning bread. The stair rail had marks of excited activity, memories of children running down the steps as the morning post arrived through the letterbox.

The bedrooms were all but lost to the outside elements, except for a small wooden footlocker that sat in a corner of a room. Inside it lay a black family Bible, but not like the new ones you would normally see for sale. It wasn't tidy, big or thick with pages of maps. Instead it was small and worn, tattered around the edges.

As I flicked though its damaged pages, it shone out with the life and involvement of those reading it before. It had hand-written notes, all in differing styles. Little scribbles of thoughts and lines, connecting one verse to another in thoughtful prose. Holding it in my hands gave me an unforgettable image of that family and their journey of trust and togetherness. Next to it lay the broken ornament that beautifully recounted the words, "The Lord is my Shepherd".

As I left this house and met back up with my guide, he started to recount from his own memories the glorious accounts of seeing God move in such dramatic and marvellous ways. He told how he had heard the cries of salvation on the local streets, and the signs and wonders that declared the awesomeness of Christ to all around; the supernatural lights that would shine from the sky and the wondrous miracles that filled the streets with praise. As his story continued, I spotted a common strand that weaved through it all. The twenty-third Psalm. This well-known piece of Scripture was a common bond for many in that heaven-soaked place.

Those words were true within his life and the lives of those he was recounting – men and women of all ages and diverse backgrounds. Each one approached their Saviour in different ways, but each knew what it meant to be in His presence. Whatever visitation they were a part of, it was something they had already recognised and touched within their own lives. From the taste within their mouths, to the smell that had filled their nostrils, His embrace had awakened their senses many years earlier. His goodness and mercy had pursued them.

As Harold, my guide, so beautifully described those events that day as we stood outside that crumbled down home of love, I saw something simple and felt it imprint itself on my soul. In His presence you hear His heartbeat, you see this world in a whole new way, and you are never the same again. May our Father unsettle you with this wonderful truth too – that He is the God of miracles in the mundane.

Moments to reflect

"The Lord is my Shepherd,
to feed, guide and shield me. I Shall not lack …
Yes, though I walk through the deep and sunless valley of the shadow of death,
I fear or dread no evil, for You are with me;
Your rod to protect and Your staff to guide, they comfort me …
Only goodness, mercy, and unfailing love shall follow me all the days of my life,
and through the length of my days
the house of the Lord and His presence shall be my dwelling place."

(Psalm 23:1, 4, 6 Amplified Bible)

"Above all kingdoms, above all thrones.
Above all wonders the world has ever known.
Above all wealth and treasure of the earth.
There's no way to measure what You're worth.
Crucified laid behind a stone.
You lived to die, rejected and alone.
Like a rose trampled on the ground.
You took the fall and thought of me.
Above all."

Above All by Michael W. Smith
Reunion © 2001

Prayer:

"All my hopes and dreams lay as a landscape before me, letting me see what I desire the most. Let the highest place in me be this hunger: to simply reside with You. Content in Your dwelling place, may all things flow from that place. Thank you that I am continually in Your embrace and that I can never be the same, because You have met with me."

Note from the Author

Thank you for taking the time to read through this work. It's been a journey of many conversations and prayers to find an appropriate way of giving honour and respect to the wonderful values of such Christ-filled lives.

No matter the style or number of chapters, this space could never adequately reflect the depth of beauty these lives carry. Words seem are a pale substitute for their experience of life or the personal memories that reside in those who knew them in differing ways.

In such a small book, the desire to record all individuals from every denomination and expression of our faith is superseded by the reality of choosing but a few to speak about. For those who do find their steps recorded here, they are but a few of the countless lives that deserve our learning ear – diverse expressions of truth that are gloriously sown into the wider tapestry of His great love.

There is a wonderful peace to know that there is no book large enough except that which resides in the Throne Room itself, faithfully recording each character's journey and worshipful service to their Lord and community. Its tone and style leaves all human attempts in its shadow, as it speaks so dramatically of the value of each of our lives. I pray this work encourages us to never forget that.

Finally, the twenty-nine chapters you have just read may have been recorded by my hands, but it was not written by myself. It was shaped by the interviews, readings and timeless truths discovered by many pilgrims of His love who discovered the miraculous in the mundane, who all contributed to the symphony of God's love. Indeed, I am acutely aware of the contradiction of my own name appearing with theirs!

Finally, I would love to give an open invitation to begin a conversation with you and hear about your life's steps – to learn from your insights of faith and hear your God-stories that hold such priceless worth. Below are some contact details. Please feel free to get in touch. We are all fellow travellers, carriers of His wondrous truth and seekers of the extra-ordinary.

Email me at AndyS@integrityeurope.com